Not rev'
DR

Historic Musselburgh

*The Official Publication of the Com-
mittee appointed to carry through the
Ceremony of Riding the Marches of
the Burgh of Musselburgh, 1919.*

Historic Musselburgh

BY

JAMES WILKIE

WITH MAP

William Blackwood and Sons
Edinburgh and London

1919

NOTE.

THE Author desires to acknowledge the ungrudging assistance he has received in the compilation of these pages. To all to whom he is in any way indebted, and they are too numerous for individual mention, he gives his thanks. He has consulted every work known to him to bear on the history of the Burgh and Parish; but it is deemed undesirable to burden such a book as this with references. He is content, therefore, to express his general indebtedness to the writers who have preceded him, and to others he may have quoted but refrained from naming.

In the interval that elapsed between

the writing of the earlier parts and the
last, there passed away, to the sorrow of
the community, Mr Robert Millar, Beggar
Bush, Provost of Musselburgh when the
Riding of the Marches was planned for
August 1914. No one was more deeply
interested than he in everything that
concerned the history and the welfare of
his native town. He took a most active
part in the arrangements for the ceremony. The inception of the idea of such
a volume as is now given to the public
was his, and he made many suggestions
as to its scope. It is only fitting that
his services should be referred to here.

The Map has been prepared by Mr
Millar's successor in the Provostship, Mr
William Constable, Architect, to whom,
and to the Reverend Dr Edie, Minister of
Inveresk, who did him the service of
reading the proofs, the Author would also
express his indebtedness.

CONTENTS.

APPENDIX.

I.

THE HISTORY OF MUSSELBURGH AND INVERESK

THE HISTORY OF MUSSELBURGH AND INVERESK.

PART I. FROM THE EARLIEST TIMES TO THE BATTLE OF PINKIE.

FROM its situation so near the Capital and on the usual route of invading armies, few parishes can boast a more stirring history than Inveresk. Nor for reasons that will appear can any district of Scotland claim a grander past ere yet England, that "Auld Enemy," was a nation. Here it is only possible to recall the more notable tableaux time has set between the slopes of Fawside Hill and the wide plain of the sea; between the Raven's Heugh and the burn on whose banks you now seek in vain the Chapel of S. Mary Magdalene.

Inveresk grew up around its holy hill;

Eskmuthe or Musselburgh originated at
the effluence of the river, deep and strong-
flowing then, where above the sandy bank
the coracles of the daring fishermen, who
adventured the often stormy waters of
the Firth, lay beneath the huts of mud
and wattle, and on the bent the nets were
spread to dry. Still the parish has kept
the names the old Celtic people gave her
long before the Saxon set his foot within
her boundaries, and undeterred by the
immortal wrangle of antiquaries over such
vexed questions as the sole surviving
Pictish word, there have been those who
ingeniously interpreted Musselburgh in its
primal form as the Walled Town of that
much-discussed race.

However that may be, S. Michael's
Mount acquired its sanctity in ages ante-
cedent to the dawn of recorded history.
At the coming of Christianity the

> ". . . gentle Michael of the White Steed,
> Who subdued the dragon of blood
> For love of God and the Son of Mary,"

gave his name to many an eminence on which the fire had burned to a Celtic or an Iberian deity—Manannan, Lord of the Sea, may be; or Bel, the Lord of Light; and always near the Mount was the sacred grove. Dr Thomas Ross has pointed out the frequency of dedication to the Archangel on Roman sites. But it is arguable that the solution may be found in a still higher antiquity. The practical and unimaginative Romans borrowed their gods from Greece, or adopted those of the conquered races. And when they chanced upon a spot already holy, what more natural than to choose from out their pantheon the deity they deemed most akin to him who there was worshipped? Even as Apollo and Mithra possessed certain of the characteristics of S. Michael so did earlier Celtic divinities.

The centuries are as a mist that rolls away. It is night; but the night is far spent. The moon and the stars look down upon the hill-top from the unclouded sky of early summer. The primeval forest, the *Silva Caledonia* of the Romans, stretches away to the south, and through it flows the river with impetuous current, silvered by the moonbeams where you catch the sparkle of its waters. Here and there is treacherous morass where Will-o'-the-Wisp is wont to flit with his lanthorn, and from over which the cry of the curlew mingles with the rush of water and the sough of the wind in a triad of the oldest and the saddest sounds the world hears; oldest and saddest, even as the most remote Celtic music borne down the æons of time is a weird death-croon. From the depths of the wood, where the fierce boar and the wild white cattle roam, comes at intervals the long dismal howl of the wolf.

Gradually, with the first shiver of morning, the faint dawn breaks, and from out the twitter the blackbird's liquid note floats clear, while the lark loses itself in an ecstasy of song in the blue of heaven. From the grove on the river's bank, as the morning star begins to pale and the dreaming woods emerge from shadow, there ascend to the brow of the hill to tend the sacred fire a band of white-robed, long-haired, bearded priests of the pre-Roman religion. Oak-leaves crown their brows, on the arm of each dully gleams a golden circlet. There on the Fairy Mound, remembered till last century, and now levelled and included in the new church-yard, they kneel, their faces turned, as the gaze of mankind has ever done in adoration, toward the East. The first level shaft of the rising sun strikes from the ridge across the intervening plain, and a mystical chant is borne upon the breeze, as with widespread arms the Druids greet the light. The holy fire springs into new life as the secret rite is performed. Strange foreshadowing of a diviner truth ! "Out of the immeasurable heaven He had come, in His golden chariot. Now in the wonder and majesty of His love, He was reborn upon the world."

The generations pass and the hill-summit sees another sight. Rumour has it that a strange people, beneath whose feet the known world lies prostrate, a people invincible as the sun himself, are moving northward. By-and-by the watchers see the flashing of helmet and shield on the distant slope, as in a gleaming thread the Roman soldiers come marching indomitably on into the uncharted regions of the unknown, their camp at Newstead a day's journey behind them. On they press, by what we now call Borthwick and Temple and Sheriffhall, heading straight for the coast. As suddenly the Firth is darkened with war-galleys bearing supplies of all kinds for the army. The practised eye of the Roman general at once grasped the possibilities of the Hill of Inveresk, commanding as it does that wide sweep of country from far up the Esk Valley on the south to the unexplored swamps and forests of Pictavia, in whose foul air, it was said, no living thing could breathe;

and from the farthest summit of the Pentlands to Gullane Point; the long arm of the sea beneath, with the vessels ever within hail. It was in the summer of one of the late years of the first century of our era that Agricola reached the *Sinus Bodotria*—the Firth of Forth. Rome had attained the culminating point of her autumn glory under Vespasian. The Capitol was restored, the Colosseum built, peace reigned, learning and the arts flourished, even Palestine was pacified.

Soon an impregnable fortress rose above the Esk. Eastward from the citadel, sloping to the sea along the face of Inveresk Hill, lay the Colonia, peopled by the legionaries, by Roman soldiers from all parts of the Empire, and auxiliaries from Spain and Gaul, while beyond the river and between it and the harbour was the Municipium, in which dwelt the natives of the land. The stream was spanned by the bridge of which it is not unlikely some portion is concealed by the masonry of the mediæval structure we tread to-day. Across it passed a strange and picturesque throng, coming and going, speaking tongues as diverse as their raiment, and as foreign as their faces. What visions rose before the eyes of the legionaries on guard on either bank ? The stream, clear in summer drought, or red and swollen in the winter spate, may have become the tawny Tiber, rushing like a steed unbroken through the imperial city of palaces and temples, the mistress of the world. And they might discern far on the horizon, across the Campagna,

"Where the quiet end of evening smiles,
          Miles on miles,"

the distant mountains so famous in Rome's beginning. Or it might be the sunburnt uplands of Spain or the green meadow-land of Gaul, with its willow - shaded waters ; or even the arid sands and stately palm-trees of the Orient.

The stones which the Roman builders

dressed can yet be detected in abundance,
not only in the walls of the church itself
but in Inveresk and Newbigging. It is
impossible to mistake the diagonal broach-
ing that seems as clear as when it left
those hands so long mouldered into dust.
The pavements that they laid still extend
along the ridge to Pinkieburn, though
concealed now ; and in the Shire Haugh
to the south-west, little more than a
century and a quarter has passed since
the evidence of strong entrenchments remained, and old people remembered the
Roman road that ran from the harbour
thither.

Near the spot on which our Celtic ancestors worshipped there was erected an
altar to Apollo Grannus, the long-haired
Apollo, perhaps called Apollo Grynæus
from the little town in far Æolia where
the Grove was dedicated to him.

About eleven centuries after the last
legionary left Scotland there was discovered within the grounds of Eskgrove,

in the days when beautiful, unhappy Mary
ruled the land and early in the year of
her marriage with Darnley, what Thomas
Randolph, the English Ambassador, describes as a cave. In his second letter,
that to Sir William Cecil, he quaintly
says : " The Cave found besyde Muskel-
bourge seemeth to be some monument of
the Romaynes by a stone that was found
with these words graven upon hym,
Apollini Granno Q. L. Sabinianus, Proc.
Aug. Dyvers short pillers, sette upryt
upon the grounde, covered with tyle stones
large and thyucke, torning into dyvers
angles, and certayne places lyke unto
chynes to avoid smoke. This is all that I
can gather thereof." Camden makes the
discovery take place in the year of Pinkie
Cleuch, but that is nonsense. Part of
what was discovered was, of course, a
portion of the hypocaust, such as is to
be seen to-day, but the cave may possibly
have been of even deeper interest. The
Queen at once sent a boy, to whom two

pence were given for his services, "to the Baillies of Mussilburgh," charging them to take diligent heed for the preservation of "the monument of grit antiquitie." The worthy magistrates had much to distract them in the days of the surrender at Carberry Hill and amid the welter of the wars of the Reformation, and maybe regarded the cave, like other things they did not understand, as "a monument of idolatrie." At any rate by 1593 it, together with its contents, was "utterlie abolished." But later discoveries from 1765 onward—into which, fascinating subject to the antiquary though it be, this is not the place to go in detail—amply prove that scientific excavation of the Hill of Inveresk would yield results as rich as those which repaid the investigations at Newstead.

The camp, in the words of "the sweet heathen of Monkbarns," was a *castra stativa*—a permanent military station as distinguished from a *castra æstiva*—

"things confounded by too many of our historians." In fancy we can hear Scott's immortal Antiquary discoursing in the Prætorium, certain, no doubt, as many have been since, that the mound in the churchyard was a Roman fortification ; leading his victims to the Roman bath of two rooms discovered in 1783 in the grounds of Inveresk House ; gloating over a medal of Trajan "Optimus," the Emperor born in Spain, the Pontifex, some of whose work, like the Bridge at Alcantara and the Arch at Ancona, still defies the ravages of time ; or over that aureus of Vespasian found beside a cinerary urn. We can listen to his narrative of how Agricola set forth on his campaigns against the Picts beyond the Firth, and how the guard on the hill watched the legions disappear across the Ferry and so on to Lochore, where the famous Ninth narrowly escaped annihilation, and finally to Mons Grampius or Graupius, a locality as mysterious to scholars as the burial-place of Moses, even

though Sandy Gordon placed it without
question a mile short of the Kirk of
Comrie ; a Fife colonel at Strathmiglo ;
and a later chronicler in Forfarshire, unfortunately for Monkbarns omitting to
localise it in that county at the Kaim of
Kinprunes.

The mightiest of earth's empires cease
to be. The fierce young nations of the
North were soon to clamour at the very
gates of senile Rome, and Alaric the Goth
to sack the Eternal City. The legions disappear from Scotland for ever, and with
their going thick darkness falls. Did there
pass with them the worship of Apollo and
that Persian cult of Mithraism which, introduced into the Empire through the annexa-
tions of the Cæsars in Assyria, Cappadocia,
Pontus, and Cilicia, began to spread until
it had permeated the whole army and
under the Antonines instantly burst into
prominence everywhere like a smouldering
fire that suddenly leaps into brightness ?
Almost ere the historian suspects its pres-

ence it wraps the whole world of Rome in the flame of its altars; all but Greece, whose genius was antagonistic to ideas of the East. For a time Mithraism fought a death struggle with Christianity. Like the religion of the Cross, it appealed first to the lowest—the slave—the alien—the freedman, but ere long in the person of Commodus it conquered the throne itself. It almost seemed, so far as human judgment is concerned, that it must prevail. If no Mithraic remains have been discovered on the hill of Inveresk, it may probably be taken for granted excavation would bring them to light. Along Hadrian's Wall they have been found in numbers. Whether the mysterious Cave may not have been a Mithraeum; whether the Fairy Well in Inveresk House grounds may not have been associated with the ceremony of the *taurobolium*, or baptism in the blood of a bull, is question for legitimate speculation. And whatever be the secret of the Fairy Fountain, we know, at least, that in all the religions of the old world there was to be found beside the temple of the god a holy spring, the uprising of whose limpid waters no drought could arrest, and by whose side the devout made their petitions and laid their offerings.

That the always pious and sometimes superstitious legionary who, born in lands loved of the sun, adored the light and the heat, there paid his homage to Mithra, to the *Sol Invictus* of Aurelian, is unquestioned. It was the sunset of the Roman Empire, but a sunset worthy of her slow - breaking dawn and her resplendent day ; and he who in our time has made Parnesius sing a song to Mithra, has put into the mouth of the singer things truer than that simple warrior knew :—

"Mithras, God of the Sunset, low on the Western main
Thou descending immortal, immortal to rise again !
Now when the watch is ended, now when the wine is drawn,
Mithras, also a soldier, keep us pure till the dawn !

B

Mithras, God of the Midnight, here where the great
    bull dies
Look on thy children in darkness. O take our sacrifice!
Many roads thou hast fashioned : all of them lead to
    the light,
Mithras, also a soldier, teach us to die aright!"

.   .   .   .   .   .

At length the gloom lightens a little and
we grope among the shadows. The Roman
station is deserted. With the recall of the
legions and of the fleet Inveresk has relapsed into quietude.

The Picts break through the walls of
Antonine and Hadrian ; the Britons call
in the Anglo-Saxons, and the Northmen
ravage the country. The Hill is covered
with buildings gradually going to ruin.
Nature is slowly winning back to herself
much that has been taken. The grass
grows on the causeways, the tall weed
waves in the wind from stately masonry
on which rain and tempest, frost and sunshine, are working their will. Doubtless
those vast silent chambers, those deserted
fortifications, those graves of the soldiers

beneath the rampart, those altars and caves dedicated to strange gods, are places to be avoided, haunted by evil spirits and, after nightfall, by the shades of the departed. The owl hoots eerily from the ivied gables, the bat has its abode in dark corners.

But ere long the hill awakes again.

The date at which the Kirk of S. Michael succeeded the Roman Praetorium is uncertain. That it owed its origin directly or indirectly to what is now Ireland is not a very audacious assumption. For Ireland, where the Imperial Eagles never flew, was during the early centuries of our era the sanctuary of learning, the refuge of the arts, the wellspring of literature and philosophy. It was the great missionary centre. For long this extraordinary phenomenon of a remote island on the utmost verge of Western Europe, its shores washed by stormy seas, standing as a radiant beacon amid Cimmerian darkness, puzzled every scholar.

Only the other day there was revealed a writing of the sixth century which helps to solve the problem. It relates how, before the desolation of the Empire was completed by the Vandals, the Goths, and the Alans, all the literati fled, " and in Hiberia (Hibernia ?) brought about a very great advance in learning." These scholars were generally Christians with some pagan traditions, which exactly accords with the character of the early literature of Erin.

Was, then, S. Michael's at Inveresk one of the Seven Churches founded by S. Modwenna (Darerca) of Ireland, who was the friend of S. Bride, and who died on the day on which S. Columba was born (521), or must the honour be given to S. Margaret's Chapel in the Castle ? " Apud Edinburgh in Montis cacumine in honorem Sancti Michaelis alteram aedificavit Ecclesiam." Edwin, who is said on rather doubtful authority to have founded Edinburgh, began to reign in 618, a century later ; but even if we were prepared to accept the derivation it would not affect the argument.

On the other hand, was the erection of that first Christian Church due to S. Baldred, the disciple of "S. Kentigern truly called Mungo"—*i.e.*, the dear one—who founded Glasgow? The district is mentioned by Simeon of Durham in the seventh century: "Et tota terra quae pertinet ad monasterium Sancti Baltheri quod vocatur Tyningham a Lambermore usque ad Escemuthe."

However it may be, there somehow came with sandalled feet along the moss-grown Roman way, or by some forest path, a band of monks. Keen eyes with the light of devotion in their depths gazed steadily from ascetic weather-beaten faces as, in their long robes of undyed wool, the hood thrown back over their shoulders, they saw before them the eminence crowned with majestic remains. With the rites of the Celtic Church they took possession of it in the name of their Master. Probably they were content that the fane they constructed should be of timber from the Shire wood, like S. Peter's at York, that notable Roman city; or even of wattle and mud thatched with reeds, from the great marsh of the Shirehaugh to the south-west, as was S. Columba's Monastery at Iona, built about the same time. Equally difficult of solution is the problem when first the summit knew that more enduring edifice demolished during the barbarous age of the early nineteenth century to make way for what is assuredly the least picturesque erection that ever stood on the hallowed spot. It seems certain that the mediæval S. Michael's was built from the ready - hewn Roman stones. That these determined the site, as has been suggested, is not to be believed. Other and nobler motives influenced the ancient Church.

According to Dr Carlyle, who preached in it till the last, and never lifted his voice within its successor, it consisted of a nave with double aisles. At the period of the battle of Pinkie it may have been cruciform with single aisles, though this is very doubtful. The Reformation succeeded Somerset's invasion too closely, and the Protestants did not concern themselves with enlarging. Their difficulty was to rescue from the pillage and the desolation sufficient to carry on service at all — though an important place like Inveresk, so near the capital, suffered less than remote districts, some of which practically relapsed into paganism. At the west end, in the centre of the nave, was a round turret, and to the south, and projecting slightly beyond the first aisle, was a square tower. In a sketch dated in the memorable year 1547, a southern porch is shown, and it would appear there was also a northern, ordered by the Council to be levelled in 1708. This was the side which was under the jurisdiction of the burgh; the other half was in charge of the landward heritors. We

know that old S. Michael's in 1803 had
thirteen outside doors, a most curious
feature.

That mediæval church with its pillared
aisles, one of them terminating in the
Lady Chapel, its roof lined with oak,
curiously and elaborately carved into
flowers and figures, metaphorical dragons
and winged cherubim, its flagged floor
under which the dead lay, its side altars,
each endowed by private benefaction, where
mass was sung for the souls of those who
had passed from the stormy Scotland of
old years, its images of the Blessed Virgin
and the Saints and its great High Altar
richly adorned, was the mother of many
subsidiary foundations,—of the Chapel of
S. Mary Magdalene in the grounds of
New Hailes; of the now almost forgotten
S. James's, which stood at the west end
of the mid-raw of Musselburgh looking
out upon the market - place, the Town
Cross and the Tolbooth; of another whose
very name has gone into oblivion, but

which stood somewhere at the west of the market-gate (Market Street); probably also of that at Cousland, on the southern border of the present parish; and not unlikely still another, dedicated to S. Clement, the patron of sailors and fishermen, on the slope of the rising ground to the eastward. The Vicar of Muscilburg served the cure under the Abbey of Dunfermline, along with Chaplains endowed by private bequests.

The old church on the hill saw many a stirring and splendid ceremony; its atmosphere was laden with the prayer and thanksgiving of centuries; a benedictal calm brooded within its consecrated walls.

Ere the advent of S. Margaret the Church of Scotland in its Celtic form had fallen from its pristine purity and vigour, much as four centuries later it was again to grow weak and corrupt. But under the wise and strong guidance of our saintly Queen it was gradually brought into conformity with "the rule of the right faith and the holy usage of the universal Church," so that in her reign, and that of the line of kings who sprang from her, turbulent Scotland enjoyed what was on the whole, despite occasional outbreaks of savagery, a golden age, and knew the truth in its purity, its fulness, and its loveliness. The stately Margaret, riding out from Edinburgh Castle, her blue eyes serene with the sweet selflessness of her white soul, may have knelt before Our Lady's Altar here, praying for her adopted people.

It was in the reign of the strong and prudent Alexander II. that David de Bernham, one of the best and most notable of the Bishops of St Andrews, he who consecrated so many churches throughout Scotland, held his famous diocesan Synod. The Ecclesia de Muskilburgh, which first appears as connected with S. Cuthbert's Holy Fane at Lindisfarne and with Tyningham, and then with St An-

drews, had been given by Queen Margaret
to her favourite Abbey of Dunfermline a
century and a half before, and thither
would come across the Queen's Ferry the
Abbot and his train, with the clergy,
regular and secular, of Fife. It is not
difficult to imagine the splendour of the
scene on that spring day in the year
1242 when High Mass was celebrated in
S. Michael's by the Bishop in presence of
the assembled dignitaries, — the solemn
chanting, the gorgeous vestments, the
swelling music, the dim and fragrant
clouds of incense ; and outside, in a
hushed calm of awe and reverence, the
crowd of burghers and of rustics kneeling with bowed heads in the unenclosed
churchyard to receive the blessing of the
great and beloved prelate as he passed
forth. Maybe some hunted fugitive was
there who had safely won the sacred pre-
cincts beyond the Sanctuary Crosses of
which tradition still tells. The spot used
to be shown just outside the south-east

corner of the present burial-ground where
such a cross was remembered.

Had the twenty-six decrees passed at
this Synod, and given in detail by Belles-
heim, been strictly adhered to in the
century preceding the Reformation, Scotland would have been spared much blood
and many tears.

S. Michael's saw a very different sight
less than two years before the battle of
Pinkie, when George Wishart of Pitarrow,
after a pilgrimage of passion through Fife,
preached twice within its walls, thanks to
the extraordinary tolerance — or laxity—
which the Church showed in that crisis of
her history. In all probability the two-
handed sword, which was usually borne
before him by Knox or another, made its
appearance. He was certainly attended
by the lairds of Longniddry and Ormiston
and other armed admirers. Crichton of
Brunstane, the accommodating traitor who
had shortly before this offered to Henry
VIII. to arrange for the murder of Beaton

on extremely moderate terms, clanked up
the floor with the rest. The Cardinal,
by far the ablest Scottish statesman of
his day, was barbarously slain five months
later, and, ere that, Wishart had been
tried and burnt opposite the Castle Gate
of St Andrews. Whether he be held
martyr or English spy, or something of
both, depends on our reading of history
and point of view. The company he kept
is not a certificate of patriotism or honour.

In S. Michael's the congregations were
large, a contrast to the apathy of Haddington, where Wishart prophesied a lurid
destiny for the light-hearted town, because
to hear "God's Messenger," as he fondly
imagined himself, one hundred persons
could not be brought together, while
thousands flocked to witness one of the
stage - plays that were so favourite an
amusement. "Fire and sword shall reach
thee : strangers shall possess thee, and
thine own inhabitants shall be driven
forth or made to serve in bondage." Fire

and sword and the rest duly arrived at
the hands of his friends the English, as
was not unfrequently the case during
several centuries, and the prophecy was
fulfilled. Unfortunately for the reputation of the prophet, it is a fact, however
disappointing, that the more godly, or
more curious, town of Musselburgh fared
no better.

Great and Little Inveresk were inured
to the passage of armies and familiar with
the clank of mail. Forty-four years before
De Bernham's Synod, "Muskelbruch beside
the sea" had witnessed a great gathering
of "the mychty Lordys of Scotland" to
swear allegiance to the son of William,
whose banner first bore "the ruddy lyon
ramped in gold," whose brother founded
the Abbey of Lindores, and whose widowed
Queen Ermengarda that of Balmerinach.
In 1314 the fugitive chivalry of England,
broken on the field of Bannockburn, fled
across the bridge, or through the ford,
and passed beneath S. Michael's Kirk in

little better order than the Hanoverian dragoons when Prince Charlie scared them at Corstorphine. And a quarter of a century earlier it had echoed to the thud of two hundred horse when in 1290 Sir William Wallace cantered from the Figgate Moor to the capture of Dunbar.

It experienced the horrors of that Burnt Candlemas when the army of Edward III. sent up in flame every village between the Borders and Leith, and even the Lamp of Lothian was not spared. The tide of war flowed so often through the quaint old town, and the red cock crowed so frequently within its gates, that it is little wonder no building now stands to take us beyond the sixteenth century. Yet if the richly adorned church, consecrated by so many memories, in which our fathers served God, must needs go, a dwelling was spared until between 1820 and 1830 which might well have been left, if but as an ancient monument. It was a one-storey cottage with walls three feet thick, and it occupied

a position immediately to the north-west of
Pinkie, where the first house in the High
Street now is. It contained two rooms
with vaulted ceilings, and at the door was
a broad stone seat on which one might sit
and view the life of the old road that led
south-east. In 1332, eighteen years after
Scotland finally won her independence, it
was the best lodging the ancient burgh
could boast. Musselburgh might well have
been proud to protect those hoary walls,
after S. Michael's her most valuable possession. The old church had gone, Loretto
had gone, the bridge, in its present form,
certainly dates no further back than what
is known as the pre-Reformation period—
that of the first four Jameses; the most
venerable of the abodes in Inveresk present
externally the aspect of excellent specimens
of Scottish domestic architecture of the sixteenth and beginning of the seventeenth
centuries, though internal evidence and the
traditional association of the monks of New-
battle with them indicate earlier origin.

But that time - worn dwelling at Pinkie
Gate probably stood there when the Sair
Sanct ruled, and in it died six centuries
ago the companion in arms of King Robert
the Bruce and the Good Lord James, Randolph, Earl of Moray, Regent of Scotland,
that "very parfite knight" who, as Sir
Walter Scott conjectures, may have been
the hero of the old ballad known in so many
variants, "Lord Randal my Son." He it was
who had sent Roger of Fawside, the strong
tower on the braehead above Wallyford,
as Ambassador to the Court of Edward.
According to Wyntoun, Randolph had been
poisoned at a feast at Wemyss Castle on
the opposite shore, and the Breve Chronicle
amplifies the story to the effect that an
English friar, instigated by Edward Balliol,
had introduced a cankered confection which
did its work so slowly that he had been
able to escape. Lord Hailes, one of our
most reliable historians, but in this instance
following Boece, one of our most imagina-
tive, combats the suggestion of foul play,

C

and alleges that the Regent had been
suffering from an incurable disease. Be
that as it may, at a crisis in Scottish
history when his removal was of the
greatest importance to England, Randolph
was taken so ill near Wallyford that he
could proceed no further and was brought
back here.   The kingdom had been
weakened by the death of the heroic Bruce
three years before : Balliol and the disin-
herited lords were preparing invasion, and
Edward III. only waited till strife broke
out to step in and reap the advantage.
The Regent's was the most precious life in
the country. The citizens of Musselburgh,
quaint figures we should think them now,
took turns in watching over him. The
magistrates mounted an informal guard of
honour before the house. But his illness was
mortal, and he passed away on the 20th of
July 1332. His body was solemnly borne
with chant and dirge up the slope to S.
Michael's Kirk, where, before the high altar,
it lay in state, watched night and day
by the cowled monks, while the tapers

round the bier threw deep and wavering shadows among the aisles as the darkness closed in.

His successor in the Regency, Donald, Earl of Mar, nephew of King Robert, wished to reward the devotion of the burghers. They declined; they had only done their duty. "Sure you are a set of honest fellows"—with singular precision the words of Mar have come down to us. From that day the Honest Toun has proudly borne "Honestas" as its motto. So runs the tradition. Virtue did not go materially unrewarded after all. Mar conferred upon the burgh the right to certain dues, which ceased only when the Roads and Bridges Act came into operation.

The centuries pass on.

Towards the close of a December day in the year 1543, while the Commons still mourned the early death of the Gude Man o' Ballingeich, heartbroken by the treachery and ingratitude of the fierce and mercenary nobles, a little company of dismounted knights and men-at-arms appeared, escorting a few ladies, at the same bridge that to-day spans the Esk. The river went roaring down in winter spate, dun and wrathful: the lowering clouds betokened snow, and the cold wind came driving up the Firth, where the white caps of the waves flashed against the murky sky. The warder of the gate that then filled the arch-way came running from the guardhouse on the other side to find a body of pilgrims on their way to the holy shrine of Our Lady of Loretto, first for the time among the sacred places of Scotland. Onward they came, all humbly and on foot, as befitted their pilgrimage, yet not without a tell-tale dignity of mien that made the man, even before he saw the royal bearings, bend unconsciously in low obeisance. And, in truth, seldom have prouder feet trodden that venerable bridge, "over which," ac-cording to Dr Robert Chambers, "all of noble or kingly birth that approached Edinburgh for at least a thousand years must have passed: which has witnessed

the procession of monks, the march of
armies, and the trains of kings: which
has rattled beneath the feet of Mary's
ambling steed, and thundered beneath the
war-horse of Cromwell," and which in the
last and most romantic episode of the
Stewarts' fascinating story vibrated under
the elastic tread of Prince Charlie's Highland host. For the central figure was none
other than Mary of Lorraine, the widowed
queen of James V., the Regent who, more
than her beautiful and martyred daughter,
or even perhaps than Knox himself, was by
her policy to determine the fate of the
ancient order and of the ancient Church.

Up in S. Michael's, where the monks
were chanting compline, the lights began
to glimmer; but ere the darkness deepened,
the royal party were skirting the woods of
Pinkie, where rose the square tower that
marked the fortalice of the Abbots of Dunfermline. A little later, in the dim light
of the shrine, the queen mother knelt
before the altar with its gilded crucifix,

above which gleamed the letters I.N.R.I. All was still save the sough of the wind as it moaned among the branches its warning of the gathering storm, and, far off, the thunder of the surge upon the shore. What were the orisons uttered to the Blessed Virgin in those weeks ere the Queen passed thence to Stirling to keep Yule we partly know, and partly we can guess.

"Praying for peace among the lordis, and with the realm of England," says the old chronicler, "she remainit thair twentie days in her prayeris."

"Praying for peace with the realm of England!" Was any prophetic vision vouchsafed of that dark day not four years later, when English cannon stood beside S. Michael's Kirk and the Esk was red with blood and choked with corpses?

"Praying for peace among her lordis!" Did there rise before her no monitory figure, in stature a little below the average, yet well-proportioned, broad-shouldered, dark-

visaged and black-bearded, bearing himself
with natural dignity and majesty of car-
riage, his eyes flashing when excited, with
the conviction of the man who never doubts
his own inspiration : the figure of Knox, who
was to work such dule to the fated Stewart
line : between whom and her house no truce
could ever be set, for between them lay the
gulf that separated the old order, as well as
the old religion, from the new ?

The famous chapel had but a short
history. Despite the opinion that long
prevailed to the contrary, it would appear
to boast no higher antiquity than the reign
of James V. On 29th July 1534 a Charter
was granted to a hermit, Thomas Duthy, or
Douchtie, and his successors of a piece of
land in the territory of Musselburgh "*pro
edificatione unius capellae, in honorem Dei
omnipotentis et Beatae Mariae de Laureto*."
This Laureto is Loretto in Italy from which
Thomas, "quha haed been lang Capitane
befoir the Turk, as was allegit," brought
"ane Ymage of Our Lady," as is recorded

in the 'Diurnal of Remarkable Occurrents.'
It soon sprang into high repute. James,
who, like his father of the Iron Belt, went
much on pilgrimage, came hither on foot in
1536 shortly after its erection. · He had
set out for France in July to speed his suit
for Marie de Bourbon, but had encountered
such stormy seas as to render the continuation of the voyage impossible. He accordingly returned, and in August undertook
this journey to seek the blessing of Our
Lady ere he adventured again. "*Hodie
soluto disjeunio dominus Rex pedestre pere-
grinavit de Stirling versus Sanctam Mariam
de Laureitt et pernoctabat in Edinburgh.*"
Few there are now, gentle or simple, whose
devotion is so strong as to impel them to
walk from Stirling to Edinburgh on one
day. James essayed the voyage again on
1st September and reached France safely.
It was not Marie he married there on the
1st day of January 1536-7, but the fair
and delicate Madeline.

James Grant, that wonderful compendium

of historical learning and traditionary lore, devotes three chapters of one of the best of his romances to Loretto. Unfortunately much poetic licence must in this instance be allowed to his record. He only exaggerated the errors of his authorities. The hermitage does not appear to be connected with the Convent of S. Catherine at the Sciennes, though possibly it may have been visited by the Sisters : it certainly had not " been built in an age anterior to all written record," nor did it enjoy its " ancient fame —pure and undefiled " in the days of James III., who was murdered in the mill near Sauchieburn long before the Hermit set out on his adventurous career in paynim lands.

Hertford, who had no respect for the stately and beautiful Border abbeys, could not be expected to spare a chapel which enjoyed a reputation so great as this, and, like the Tolbooth which its stones were to build and repair at a later date, it was partially destroyed in 1544, to be reconstructed and to survive until the cataclysm of the

Reformation finally overwhelmed it with so much more.   Dr Carlyle tells how, according to the report of masons living in his day, the steps of the old stair leading up to the Town House were the bases of the pillars of the chapel.

Sir David Lyndsay of the Mount near Cupar, who knew the Lothians as well as he knew Fife, exercised his pungent humour—

> " The flash of that satiric rage
> Which bursting on the early stage
> Branded the vices of his age,
> And broke the keys of Rome "—

on the pilgrimages " to adore ane image in Laureit " in those last melancholy years of the outlived order, and Lord Glencairn's " Epistil direct fra the halie Hermeit of Alareit to his Brethern the Gray Friars " is to be found approvingly incorporated in Knox's entertaining History.   The story of the miracle in 1558 is too well known to need repetition.

The only trace of the chapel now remaining, or of the hermit's cell, is the cellar under the mound. Dr Moir records that a number of human skulls were found beneath the earthen floor in 1831. A stone with the date 1647, a coronet and certain letters intertwined, is placed above the entrance. Like the Abbot's mitre over the doorway at Monkbarns, it would have formed an excellent theme for a treatise by the worthy antiquary MacCribb, who had the audacity to question the accuracy of his rival's eyesight in matters where he was prejudiced. All knowledge of its origin is buried in the green kirkyard on the hill.

And now we come to the battle,[1] which

[1] "This battell and felde now, whiche is the most principall part of my matter, y⁰ Scottes and we are not yet agreed how it shal be named. We cal it Muskelborough felde, because that is the best towne (and yet bad enough) nigh the place of oure metig. Some of thē call it Seton felde (a toune thear nie too) by means of a blynd prophecie of theirs, whiche is this or sum suche toy, Betwene Setō and the Sey, many a man shall dye that dey. Some wyll haue it Fauxside Bray, feld of the hil (for so they cal a bray) vpon the syde whearof our foreward stoode, redy to cum doune

ranks among the most notable fights in Scottish history, and is second to Flodden only as the most terrible disaster suffered by our arms. It was fought on the Feast of S. Finnian, Saturday the 10th of September 1547, almost exactly thirty-four years after the darkest day in Scottish annals, the 9th September 1513. The cause of quarrel need hardly be recalled. Henry VIII., from the moment he heard of the birth of Queen Mary, on the Feast of the Conception of the Blessed Virgin, 1542, and of the death of her father immediately thereafter, had, with the view of bringing Scotland into subjection, demanded the custody of the infant Sovereign till she was ten years of age. His idea was to wed her to his son Edward, who was also a child. He persistently intrigued to that

and joyne. Sum oother will have it Vndresk, in the fallowes whearof they stoode and we met. Sum will have it Walliford feld, and sum no feld at all, for that they say thear wear so few slain, and that we met not in a place by appointement certayn, according to the order, and maner of battell ; with such like fonde argumentes."—PATTEN.

end through the assured Lords—in other
words, the Protestant nobles in his pay.
While Beaton lived surrender was impossible. Beaton fell; but Henry profited
nothing by the long projected crime he
encouraged, for he soon followed the
murdered Cardinal. The Protector continued the rough wooing which has made
his name of Hertford hateful, and brought
on Sir Ralph Evers and Sir Brian Latoun
the bloody retribution of Ancrum Moor.

As regards the campaign of Pinkie,
though wel_nigh four centuries have passed,
we are able to follow almost every movement of the contending armies, and to
realise the scene as vividly as though we
had watched the fray from the summit of
Fa'side. Contemporary chroniclers, Scots
and English, supply the material. In the
southern army fought a Londoner, William
Patten, who from the Parsonage of S.
Mary Hill in that metropolis, sent out on
28th January 1548 his diary of "The Ex-
pedicion into Scotland." He was a learned

person, an ardent Protestant, superstitious withal in his own way, and naturally much biassed towards the English point of view. We have also our own Robert Lindesay, tenant in Pitscottie, a mile or so east of Ceres in Fife, the writer who continued the chronicles of Hector Boece without displaying the amiable credulity of that distinguished Professor of Divinity. Pitscottie finished his chronicles in 1576, and as many of his Fife neighbours took part in the war he probably gleaned his particulars from them. The accounts naturally differ in certain details, as no two eye-witnesses, even when on the same side, were ever known to give an identical version ; but it is possible to construct from the sources available a consistent narrative and to follow the movements of the armies, if the aspect of the countryside in the middle of the sixteenth century be kept in mind.

Musselburgh was then a little town, of thatched houses mostly, though a few of the buildings attained to the dignity of tile, or even of slate or stone. It was a poor place to English eyes, and one which their armies gave the inhabitants frequent opportunities for reconstructing, yet picturesque with its town-house, its chapels and its monks' mills, its broad street and its mid-raw, and especially its large gardens and abundant greenery. A great expanse of links, grown over with clumps of whin and broom and fragrant with wild thyme, stretched on both sides of the river mouth, on the north-west of which ran a row of odoriferous biggings—the Fisherraw of the Chronicles. Beyond the bridge just to the west of Belfield was the Gudeman's Croft, the acre abandoned to the Devil, a place accursed, the haunt of evil spirits, and used only, if at all, for the burning of witches. The summit of Carberry was unwooded. Fa'side Tower stood quaint and strong where its sightless windows still look out over a far stretch of smiling country, " a sory castell and half a skore houses of a lyke woorthiness by yt," according to Patten, who was accustomed to the stately fortresses of England. It was to be a sorrier sight ere the English were done with it. Old S. Michael's crowned the eminence above the river as we have already described, and there is no mention of any dwelling between the cleuch at Pinkie Burn and the church, though possibly two of those now standing were then represented in some form. From Fa'side down to join the road from the bridge there came a track thirty feet broad, enclosed between two feal dykes each an ell high. Dr Moir believed that this, in its lower reach, was the vallum of the Roman Camp, the eastern bend of which came almost immediately in front of Inveresk House and was used as a common country lane. From a clump of trees looked out the fortalice of Pinkie, belonging to the Abbot of Dunfermline. It then commanded a fine view of the sea. To the east of the church Patten saw two steep conical

mounds which have entirely disappeared.
It seems impossible to agree with Delta
that these are the mounds in the churchyard, of which one remains. They were
doubtless removed by some enterprising
farmer who found them interfere with his
ploughing.

The Protector was well served by
Scottish traitors. The Laird of Ormiston,
who had attended Wishart on his appearance in S. Michael's, notified Somerset,
as recorded in State papers now acces-
sible, that the army of Scotland had
been ordered to convene on the Fallo
Muir on the last day of August; that the
Governor "goes to Newbottle to haste
to the Peaths to stand there"; that Leith
is empty and Edinburgh prepared to resist
attack. Another precious pair, Lennox
and Wharton, reported to him four days
before the battle that there is great
dissension among the nobles and no great
power assembled. The latter part of the
statement was untrue, but they were doubt-

less not far wrong when they added, "the
Governor fears his own more than yours."

Ere the blazing beacons carried north
the news that the English were about to
cross the Border, the Earl of Arran, Regent
of Scotland, had sped the Fiery Cross
even to the Western Isles and to Shetland
to summon to the muster all between
sixteen and sixty, "baith spirituall and
temporal," in their best armour and array,
"with XXX days victuall to defend the
realm fre the Englishman."

"The haill airmie of Scotland gadderit
and convenit . . . be eist Edinburgh upoun
the wast syde of the watter of Innerask
abone Mussillburgh and thair gaif thair
mustaris to the Governour. . . ."

According to Pitscottie, who ought to
know best, the army consisted of 40,000
fighting men, beside Borderers, with 12
shot of artillery and 20 small field-pieces.
Angus led the vanguard (10,000), Huntly
the rear-guard (10,000), the Regent himself "the great battell" (20,000).

The English had broken up their camp at Berwick on Sunday, September 4th, and on Monday adventured across " the Peaths," the steep glen near Dunglass which was to cause Cromwell anxious moments a century later. A greater general than Arran would probably have overwhelmed the enemy there. That such was his first intention Ormiston's letter suggests. Treachery and the fact that nearly all the lairds of the eastern Border were in the English interest probably explain his change of plan.

On Wednesday the 7th the invaders passed the Tyne at Linton Brig and camped at Longniddry, and on Thursday the 8th, being the Feast of the Nativity of the Blessed Virgin, as Patten, Protestant though he was, proudly notes, they sighted a cloud of 600 Scottish horsemen to the south hovering on their left flank upon the hillside, and keeping pace with the army " very crank and brag," taking observations and fleeing off when threatened.

Some days before, the Scots had seen a magnificent fleet of sixty-six ships—a galley and 35 caravels, low-pooped, high-waisted, gaily adorned, with 30 other vessels bearing munitions and provisions of all sorts, moving up the Firth in advance of the land forces, and for the most part coming to anchor opposite Leith. They had sailed from Berwick on the 2nd under Admiral Lord Clinton. Now they came slowly down again and took up a position from about the mouth of the Magdalene Burn past Musselburgh, with the victuallers keeping alongside the army. The anchorage was chosen so that their guns could play on the Scots if, as they did, they moved near it.

On Friday the 9th, the anniversary of Flodden, which date Patten found in his calendar marked with the name of S. Gorgon, to whom he devotes a page of ponderous ribaldry, the English pitched their camp in sight of the Scots. It extended from above Prestonpans through

Wallyford and Drummore to Musselburgh Links, and contained a force of 14,200 men, including 2000 light cavalry and 200 Spanish mounted carabineers. Tranent on the flank went up in flame, according to their practice of leaving the country behind them devastated as by a plague.

There, then, on the night before the battle, lay Somerset's army, a splendidly equipped and, for the most part, a highly disciplined force.

They saw before them on the rising ground beyond the Esk, at two miles' distance, the four great rows of white tents occupying the brae from Stoneyhill towards Edmondstone, "not unlike unto four great ridges of ripe barley." Patten describes the position as about half a mile beyond the town, and near a house which he informs us belonged to the Laird of Brimston (Brunstane). The slope was called in old days Edmondstone Edge. The banks of the river in front were high and steep, as

they still are. On the south was a great
marsh, the Shire Haugh morass, stretching
out on both sides of the Esk, which then
flowed nearer Monktonhall. Below Carberry extended a slough of black mud.
The Scots light horsemen, crossing the
river, went prancing up and down the
hill all morning, and in their eagerness
made a fatal blunder. Near Fa'side
almost the entire force was drawn into
an encounter with the chivalry of England.
The Scots on their shaggy little steeds
were overborne by the heavy and power-
fully equipped cavalry of the enemy, their
leader was sorely wounded, his son, the
Master of Hume, taken prisoner, along with
two priests and six gentlemen, and no less
than 1300 of their number were slain.
This meant, for effective purposes, the
practical elimination of the Scottish horse
from the battle that was to ensue. It
was a wild skirmish fought with des-
perate bravery. The Scots dashed up,
scattered and wheeled about shouting their

war-cries as was their wont; but instead
of enticing their foes into an ambush of 500
foot laid for them, allowed themselves to
be engaged by the whole of the southern
cavalry supported by 1000 infantry. They
fell almost to a man.

The English left was then extended
along the brae-face, and traces of the
trenches they dug may yet be seen. From
the hill Somerset and his staff overlooked
the Scots camp and then rode down
Crookston Loan. Thence the white tents
across the river showed with great dis-
tinctness. The Protector probably cantered
on till he reached the spot still marked at
the end of " The Lang Walk" in the
grounds of Eskgrove where the monument
stands. It bears the inscription, " The
Protector, Duke of Somerset, encamped
here 9th September 1547." The word
"encamped" appears to be due to a mis-
understanding. The encampment on the
9th, the eve of the battle, has already
been noted. On the 10th, which is the

date given in the note to Delta's poems,[1] the Protector encamped on Edgebuckling Edge, the slope which runs behind Pinkie Mains and so to Levenhall, and is cut through by the "new London road" at a spot where many stone coffins were found. These, of course, are of a remote date, though one ingenious writer conceives them evidence of the sepulture of the English.

According to Pitscottie, "when thay saw and spayit the Scotismen so greit ane armie

---

[1] Does Dr Moir refer to an earlier memorial, "a square pillar surmounted by an antique stone representing a fleur-de-lis"? The passage is curious. The pillar, it is said, "marks the spot where the royal tent was pitched on the eve of the battle, and bears the following inscription :—

THE PROTECTOR, DUKE OF SOMERSET,
Encamped here, 10th September,
1547.

The pillar was erected by the late Lord Eskgrove.

The stanza reads as follows :—

"Sated with blood, and glad his prey to leave,
    Five hours in hot pursuit and carnage spent,
In yon green clump, by Inveresk, at eve,
    Proud Somerset, the victor, pitched his tent:
There, 'mid its circle grey of mossy stone,
    A time-worn fleur-de-lis still marks the spot,
Which else had to the searcher been unknown ;
    For of that field one other trace is not."

and so weill orderit, they war greatly effeirit and belieffit nothing but schort battell."

As it were yesterday, we can see the Protector, the greatest noble in England, the sun flashing from his armour, riding slowly back with his splendid company of 300 horse—among them the Earl of Warwick, Lord Dacre, Lord Grey de Wilton, and Sir Ralph Sadleyr. Maybe the gallant Edward Shelley, who was to die on the morrow, was of the band. Up between the dykes they went, scarcely disturbed by an occasional shot from the Scottish cannon, which were singularly ineffective, seeing that guns had been introduced into Scotland a hundred and seventeen years earlier, three decades before they are mentioned in English history. Doubtless Somerset was discussing the feasibility of cannonading Edmonstone Edge from Crookston Loan and Inveresk Hill when a sudden bugle-blast rang out. They had reached a point near the present farm buildings at Crookston. The troop was

at once halted. A herald bearing the
Royal Arms of Scotland was seen spur-
ring up, and with him a trumpeter. The
rest rode almost out of earshot, while
Somerset and Warwick awaited the mes-
sage. It was an offer to let the invaders
return as they came, and to submit terms
of peace. The trumpeter bore a cartel from
Huntly challenging Somerset to decide the
issue by a single combat, or by a small
number on either side. Warwick would
have accepted the invitation ; the Lord
Protector rejected both proposals.

The interview was punctuated by an
occasional discharge from beyond the Esk.

Patten agrees with Pitscottie that the
Regent was determined to fight and
certain of victory, but does not mention
the letters stated by the Fife chronicler
and by Hayward to have been sent from
the English offering terms,[1] and ignored.

[1] The terms are said to have been that the English
army should withdraw from the country, provided the
infant Queen was not allowed to leave Scotland and no
agreement was made with France to bind her till she
could decide for herself as to her marriage.

Shortly before eight on Black Saturday the English struck their tents and moved forward straight on S. Michael's Kirk, with the object of placing their cannon in position along the brow of Inveresk Hill and down Crookston Loan. On the other hand, Arran seems to have formed the impression that, dismayed by the overwhelming odds, the invaders were about to attempt a retreat to the fleet from the level sands of Musselburgh. His idea was to thrust a wedge between them and the sea, and, if possible, fall upon them where they lay.

All through our national history appears a temptation to the Scottish Army to abandon a strong natural position at the last moment. At Bannockburn it was resisted, and the most memorable and momentous of our victories was achieved. At Flodden, at Pinkie, at Dunbar — in each case for totally different reasons—it was yielded to, and the darkest days in our annals were the result.

Black Saturday dawned fair — a still

and windless autumn morning, the woods
tinged with gold already, the fields in
fallow or in stubble.

Only by the bridge could Somerset
have reached the Scottish position, and
that was manned by archers and covered
by cannon.   Across it early on that
Saturday the white host of Scotland
proudly defiled — tall, fine - looking, well-
proportioned men, all clad much alike,
gentlemen and privates, in jacks covered
with white leather, doublets of white
leather or fustian, and usually white hose.
They wore no ornaments like the English, " onles cheynes of latten drawen four
or fyve tymes along the thighs of their
hosen and dooblet sleves for cuttyng."
With the rest there passed that body of
Churchmen, under the Abbot of Dunfermline or the Bishop of Dunkeld, who
bore above them the banner of white
sarcenet, whereon was painted the figure
of Holy Church, her long hair streaming
over her shoulders, kneeling before a

crucifix, and inscribed with the motto, *Afflictæ Sponsæ ne obliviscaris.*

It was a rash movement, yet but for incapacity and treachery it might have resulted in the annihilation of the English. Angus hesitated to carry it out, and only did so "under paine of treassone." He passed "ower the watter of Inverask avastetelt the kirk thaireof" (with his horse swimming or struggling through the stream), "and stude in arrayit battell in the sight of his enemies till his ost and the governour come ower the bredg to Mussillburgh and stude under and avastell [1] the kirk of Innerask and abone the fisheraw. . . ."

The sudden and almost simultaneous movement of each army disconcerted the plans of the other. There was no chance of planting English cannon on Inveresk Hill now, for the Scots already held it, and were moving round by Pinkieburn to seize the slopes of Carberry. As they

[1] In another MS. of Pitscottie, given "a eastill."

formed up, preparatory to rushing towards
the acclivity, the Master of Graham, with
a few of his men, was slain by a shot
from the fleet.   This alarmed the Highlanders,   who   were   unfamiliar   with
cannon.

The weather grew cloudy and lowering.
As the hosts prepared for battle, a hoarse
murmur as of many waters rose over the
field, even as Homer likened the Argives'
shout " to a wave on a steep shore
when the south wind cometh and stirreth
it."   The Scottish guns thundered out,
the 3000 Islesmen under Argyle shouted
their slogan—

> " And with their cries discordant mix't
> Grumbled and yelled the pipes betwixt."

The English ordnance was on the crest
of Carberry ere the Scots, moving over
the plain, could reach it ; and as Lord
Grey with his veterans, and the demi-lances
under Lord Fitz-Waters, were now ordered
to charge, the Scots division under Angus

fell into their favourite hedgehog formation—that on which, at Bannockburn, the
matchless chivalry of Edward broke like
ocean on an iron-bound shore. The front
rank, almost kneeling, grasped their pikes
in both hands, the butt-end on the ground
against the right foot, their bucklers on
the left wrist; the second rank with
their pikes over the shoulders of those
in front, crossing the points of the
others; and so on with the ranks behind. Against this impenetrable wall, and
hampered by the furrows of the fallow
field, the splendid cavalry went down and
the standard of England was barely saved,
the staff being left in Scottish hands.
Lord Grey was dangerously wounded, and
many fell. The survivors fled back to
the hillside, where the Protector anxiously
followed the course of events. The
affrighted and riderless horses carried confusion with them, and victory hovered
ready to descend. Pitscottie says Somerset prepared to seek safety in flight when

he heard it was impossible to break the
Scots where they stood "mor nor to
break ane stane wall." He adds that
Warwick threatened him as a traitor.
The master gunner of England had
fallen : the day hung in the balance.

Then in an instant the whole aspect
changed. The crisis had come when the
Scottish cavalry could have completed the
rout. But it had been almost wiped out
in Hume's rash adventure. Angus had
far outstripped Arran with the "main
battell" and Huntly with the rear-guard,
and was left without support. Warwick
seized the psychological moment and
threw the Spanish carabineers, clad in
full mail, in front of the foe. They
dashed up to the slough and discharged a
volley at short range in the faces of the
Scots pikemen ; the hagbutters supported,
and the archers now came into action
while the cannon roared. Slowly Huntly
moved his men back on the main body.
The clansmen under Argyle had, after

their manner, broken loose to plunder the English dead, and seemingly mistook this for a retreat. They had been shaken when the Master of Grahame fell; now it seemed to them a very *inferno* was raging. The flash and roar of the cannon answering each other from Carberry and Inveresk, the "great stur" that arose from the dry fallow land hiding the combatants, were bad enough; but suddenly from the darkened heavens burst a downpour of rain that rose again from the hot earth in a steaming mist, "as it had been ane tempest in the air fallen upon them." The English cavalry recovered themselves. The pikemen believed they were deserted, and swaying to and fro broke into a thousand points of steel. Arran shouted "Treason!" probably not without cause, but foolishly. A blind panic seized the whole army, as sudden and almost unaccountable terrors have been known to fall upon a multitude brave individually. The traitors in the pay of England, seeing their chance,

E

doubtless succeeded in rendering the confusion irrecoverable. Yet for a time the English deemed all lost, though they held their ground. Somerset and Warwick at first imagined the flight a feint. Then they ordered the whole army to advance. The broken Scots cast away their weapons and stripped off their armour as they fled in a mad, unreasoning delirium. The English, on their side, relieved so unexpectedly from deadly peril, knew no mercy. The sight of the naked bodies pillaged by the Highlanders recalled the field of Peniel Heugh : the pursuit became a butchery in which no quarter was given. The river and the morass which had been its defence now proved the destruction of the Scottish army as its fragments streamed off in the hope of reaching Dalkeith, Edinburgh, or Leith. Ten thousand were done to death ere that rout was over, and the water of Esk and Pinkie Cleuch were choked with the bodies of men and horses. Many were slain with the cast-off weapons; even those who tried to conceal themselves in the river-bed, clinging to the willow roots, were killed where they clung. Far over the countryside corpses were strewn like sheaves on the harvest-fields, or, as Patten puts it, "thick as a man may note the cattell grasing in a full replenished pasture." There is the usual local tradition that Pinkie Burn ran with blood for three days and three nights— the common poetical way of expressing the memory of a great slaughter. The popular sentiment as to the causes of the disaster are embodied in the couplet—

"'Twas English gold and Scots traitors wan
The field of Pinkey, but no Englishman."

It need only be added that Fa'side was burnt after a gallant defence, and that all within it perished in the flames.

PART II. FROM THE REFORMATION TO THE NINETEENTH CENTURY.

TWENTY years after the disastrous battle of Pinkie Cleuch the hill of Carberry saw another meeting of hostile armies, hardly less memorable and in its effects really more momentous than that which ended in the butchery of Black Saturday, 1547. Yet no drop of blood was shed upon the fatal field where Mary surrendered to Kirkaldy of Grange. It was exactly a month since her ill-omened May marriage. When news of it came to Halyards, Kirkaldy buckled on again, through hatred of Bothwell, the armour he was not afterwards to lay aside.

The story of the surrounding of Borthwick is well known. Bothwell escaped by the glen past Crichton Castle and the

Collegiate Kirk to Dunbar; Mary, in man's clothes, booted and spurred, followed when the siege was raised. Her supporters rallied to her flag, and she moved west upon the capital. The Lords of the Congregation marched out of Musselburgh at her coming to check her progress. The old town had undergone a transformation since Somerset met Arran. Most of it had been destroyed in the fire and pillage of 1548: the fury of the Reformation had swept Loretto into oblivion and with it the other chapels of the parish: the hermitages and shrines had been wrecked and the holy wells polluted: the crosses had been thrown down, the altars despoiled, the figures of the saints broken or defaced. S. Michael's, a melancholy monument of departed splendour, stood closed and desolate the long week through, except when some solemn fast was ordered for the sins of the nation.

On the hill-crest the Queen with her husband awaited the rebels in battle array.

Beside the grey stone on the rounded summit, then green and bare, the interview took place, and there her fate and that of Scotland was decided. Two figures stand out clear across the centuries—the young and lovely Queen, not yet twenty-five, with all the happiness of life behind her, dogged by the evil destiny of the Stewart race : the tall and courtly Knight of Grange, cast by an equally malign fate into the company of the treacherous foes of her for whom he was in later years to go to his death. Around them gleam the lances of opposing armies waiting the word to close. Then the stealthy order of the perjured Bothwell, the levelled harquebuss pointed at the unsuspecting Kirkaldy, Mary's shrill scream of horror saving the man who began life by keeping the postern gate of St Andrews Castle at the murder of the Cardinal, who ended it on a gibbet with his face against the sun, that the savage Morton might fulfil the still more savage

prophecy of Knox : the man who, never-
theless, stands out in the sordid annals of
the sixteenth century, a figure chivalrous
as chivalry then went, if enigmatical as
that of Lethington. The following of
Mary gradually melted away, till, stricken
by Bothwell's perfidy and fearful of shed-
ding more blood, she surrendered to the
one knight she trusted, while Bothwell
slunk slowly off, out of her life for ever,
to die at last a chained and raving
maniac in the dungeons of Draxholm.

The Queen and Kirkaldy rode side by
side down the road so familiar from
Patten's description of it with its turf
dykes, and so by the Roman vallum and
under the shadow of S. Michael's to the
steep and narrow bridge, thence on by
Niddry and Craigmillar, past the black-
ened ruins of the Kirk-o'-Field into the
turbulent High Street of Edinburgh,
surging like an angry sea with the fickle
mob that, swayed by false reports of the

part she played, had turned against their
Queen.

Inveresk saw Mary no more, for the way
by which she was hurried by destiny led by
Lochleven and Langside to the Solway
and Fotheringay. The gallant Seton never
faltered from her in those last hours on
Scottish soil. With what feelings did the
Earl of Dunfermline receive the ungainly,
weak-legged figure of her son, who to his
eternal shame let her suffer execution without an effort to save or to avenge?

Not the fortalice of Pinkie alone saw
that curious compound of foolishness and
wisdom, King James the Sext, when he
rode out to Inveresk. The Rev. Adam
Colt, minister of the parish, knew him
better than did most of his clerical brethren,
and sometimes more intimately than he desired. In the General Assembly of 1601
he opposed him face to face, and was rated
by the angry monarch as a seditious knave.
Yet the homely King Jamie visited his out-
spoken subject, and the chair he occupied

is still an heirloom in the Colt family. In 1606-7, when James had found England much more amenable than his ancient kingdom and its courtly Church more congenial to his hereditary bias, Adam Colt spent many months in continuous strife with the royal authority. He had been summoned from Scotland with seven other leading ministers to attendance on the Court. When the King got tired of these intractable clergy, Adam at least fared better than Andrew Melville, who was sent to the Tower; for Colt was simply ordered "too goe home and be confynit within his awin paroche at Musselburgh," —then no great hardship any more than now.

The house which was the residence of Adam Colt and his son Oliver, successive ministers of Inveresk from 1609 to 1679, was in possession of the family for between two and three hundred years. From the courtyard a stair leads to a subterranean vaulted chamber of much greater antiquity.

It is believed to have been part of an underground passage from the Roman camp to the Colonia, and a continuation of it was discovered when the road from Newbigging to Inveresk was cut in the eighteenth century. One reason for the immunity which the stout old cleric enjoyed, despite his differences with an autocratic king, was his relationship to Maitland the Chancellor, one of the Commissioners for the Plantation of Kirks, to whom went the church manors at Inveresk, with the exception of Pinkie. Through Maitland the Lauderdale family succeeded to the superiority of the burgh and the patronage of the living. In the church, beside the vestry door, is a tablet to the memory of the second Earl and only Duke. He sat as an elder in the Westminster Assembly. It would be interesting to know what share he had in framing the Confession of Faith and the Shorter Catechism. Tributes to character emblazoned on memorial stones are meant for the eye of posterity rather than for contemporaneous criticism, and it is somewhat unfortunate that more people have read 'Redgauntlet' than the swelling Latinity on the church marble. Wandering Willie only visualised the belief of the Scottish lowland peasantry in that Homeric visit of his to the Underworld.

"There was the fierce Middleton, and the dissolute Rothes; and the crafty Lauderdale; and Dalyell with his bald head and a beard to his girdle; and Earlshall with Cameron's blude on his hand; and wild Bonshaw that tied blessed Mr Cargill's limbs till the blude sprung; and Dumbarton Douglas, the twice turned traitor baith to country and king. . . . But their smiles were fearfully contorted from time to time; and their laughter passed into such wild sounds as made my gude-sire's very nails grow blue and chilled the marrow in his banes."

There still survives a monument to one of Mr Adam Colt's elders, William Smyth, Clerk of Musselburgh, and Session Clerk,

Kirk Treasurer, and general adviser to the
Session.   The stone bears the simple inscription " Fideliter Fecimus."

It is in connection with Inveresk House
and kirk and kirkyard adjoining that the
next great historic figure emerges.   Fresh
from that campaign in which he carried
fire and sword through Ireland, sparing
neither age nor sex, and inspiring the
people with such undying hatred of him
and England, that " the curse of Cromwell
on ye!" is the bitterest of expletives beyond the Irish Channel, came the Usurper
to subdue the Scots.   The situation in some
respects resembled that before Somerset's
victory : its issue was not dissimilar.   This
time the Scots possessed a great leader, the
only general in Britain competent to cope
with the invader—namely, David Leslie,
fifth son of Patrick Leslie of Pitcairlie, near
Auchtermuchty, Commendator of Lindores.
Like Alexander Leslie, the now aged Earl
of Leven, who served as a volunteer and
without command in his army, he had been

trained under Gustavus Adolphus, and it was he who really turned the day at Marston Moor when Rupert seemed on the point of carrying all before him. Leslie had vanquished Montrose, the greatest soldier of his age, at Philiphaugh. Scotland was united in support of a covenanted king, and though the Engagers had been excluded from the army, it formed a strong force fitted to encounter Cromwell's. It was inspired by a fanaticism not less intense : yet Cromwell possessed one advantage that, so far as we can judge, determined the result and delivered the enemy into his hands. In his ranks it was the officers who preached ; in Leslie's the ministers, who knew nothing of war beyond what they gathered from congenial study of the sanguinary passages of Old Testament history, dominated all. As usual there were traitor Scots—" the master-fiend, Argyle," and the infamous Laird of Warriston among them.

Cromwell entered Scotland on 22nd July

1650 by the usual route, following for the most part in the century-old footsteps of Somerset. Again a fleet kept in touch with the troops as they passed along the coast of Berwick and the Lothians. Instead of awaiting them on Edmondstone Edge, the Scots' extended line lay from Arthur Seat to Leith. The country between Musselburgh and the English Border was wellnigh deserted and cleared of all provender. The only inhabitants seen were a few aged crones garbed in white flannel.

Early on Sunday the 28th a cloud of dust betokened the approach of the enemy, and 1400 English horse under Lambert came clattering down the London Road. The main army, with Oliver at its head, marched " in the heel of them." All the men had departed from the Honest Toun, making it a desolate place in English eyes, despite that " the gude-wives," as Cromwell called them, still remained, and were employed to bake and brew till

Leslie took an opportunity when his foe was absent to call every one away, goods and gear. Stores were landed and an entrenched camp formed, while the rain beat pitilessly. Whether the mound in the kirkyard dates from this period or goes back to Roman times is a point still undecided. In 1650 Cromwell's cannon stood upon it, as Somerset's and d'Essé's had stood in the churchyard in 1547 and 1548, commanding the passage of the river. The flagged S. Michael's served to stable English horses, no spot being sacred to the sectaries. The officers took possession of the new and well-built houses of Newbigging, while Oliver himself occupied Inveresk House when he was not on the Links, where, opposite Linkfield, rose the knoll, traditionally associated with his tent. The turf from Eskmouth to Ravensheugh was almost hidden by the canvas of his lines, and a further cluster of white tents lay across the river at Stoneyhill.

The invaders got the worst of it during
the long month that Musselburgh formed
their base of operations and Dunbar their
victualling port.   The attempt to draw
Leslie failed.   The Scottish cavalry surprised the army on the Links, as Kirkaldy's
men in that brilliant raid from Edinburgh
Castle had surprised the Regent Lennox
in Stirling.   Silently the horsemen left
Leslie's camp, keeping south and crossing
the Esk far up to avoid Oliver's pickets
near the bridge and his battery on the
hill.   Tradition says they crossed the Howe
Mire by a little-known path ; more probably they kept to the south of it.   So
under the stars they rode round to Wallyford by familiar ways.   Then with a shout
of "God and the Kirk, all is Ours!" and
"King and Covenant!" they were in the
thick of the tents, slashing and cutting,
bringing down canvas, slaying and wound-
ing in the confusion as they dashed on.
It was a brigade against the most highly
disciplined and steadiest troops in the world,

and the issue could not be decisive. Cromwell, reporting, says he expected the attack, which makes its success the more wonderful. The gallant Scots had to retreat at last, but not until with little loss to themselves they had given a severe shock to Oliver's prestige. The strategy of Leslie baffled him; in vain he moved his army round to Colinton; his enemy wheeling on an inner circle was ever before him. The Lord General spent few more anxious weeks than those, and but for the fatuity that gave the Presbyterian clergy the determining voice at Dunbar, and paid heed to the fanatical injunction to "go down against the Philistines at Gilgal," the fate of the Protector might have been sealed. It was on the last day of August (Old Style) that the Ironsides struck their tents, burnt their huts, and began their retreat from Musselburgh which should have been their Moscow. Provisions had grown scanty since Leslie completed the desolation of the parish, the autumn was

F

boisterous and wet, the equinoctial gales might scatter the fleet and bring starvation. Sickness was prevalent. Sullenly Cromwell fell back, "the Peaths" at Dunglass intersecting his route. In a moment Leslie's cavalry were along the Lammermuirs and held the passes. The Scots had only to wait. The old fatal impatience that served them so ill at Flodden and at Pinkie, this time manifested through the Committee of Estates and Kirk, was their undoing. Oliver considered as to embarking his foot and trying to cut his way south with his cavalry. At the critical moment "the Lord delivered his enemies into his hand." Carlyle would fain exonerate the preachers. "The poor Scotch clergy have enough of their own to answer for in this business." As indeed they had.

Cromwell did not spare the vanquished. There was little to choose between "the poor Scotch clergy" and the Lord General when it was a question of smiting the

Philistines or slaying the Amalekites. They were happiest who fell in battle. Of the 10,000 prisoners, the most part were sold into slavery in the Plantations across the Atlantic.

Oliver Colt, who had conformed to Episcopacy in the days of King Charles the First, and was Rector of Inveresk and Musselburgh, did not remain to act as host to his terrible visitors. He fled to the protection of the Royalists, but is said to have paid a secret visit to his house during the temporary absence of the intruders, and to have experienced adventures such as are usually found in the historical novel. In the privately printed ' History of the Colt Family,' the author, Captain Colt, tells the most curious tale of all. In 1789 the laird of that day, Robert, when making improvements, removed some old panelling. The entrance to the long-forgotten secret passage was revealed. Those concerned at once entered, and, following it to a point immediately under the room used by

Cromwell, came, to their amazement, upon a cavalier in full armour sitting beside a keg of gunpowder with hand outstretched towards it. The clothes crumbled into dust at a touch, revealing the skeleton beneath. It was conjectured to have been that of the younger brother of Oliver Colt, who, when the minister left, may have gone into concealment with the object of ridding Scotland of her arch-enemy. The guesses were many and conflicting, and the story remains a mystery of the venerable, ghost-haunted house.

It was another and less stately dwelling that served as the abode of the long line of notable men who followed the Colts in serving the cure of Inveresk and Musselburgh. The vicarage of pre-Reformation days stood in the vicinity of the present manse. It seems to have passed to the Burgh some time after the upheaval of 1560. At any rate in 1627 the minister received " ane hundredth pounds yearly of ye Towne of Musselburgh ffor ye Vicarage." The Vicar's Well

stood in the Dambrae till comparatively
recent years.   The vicarage itself seems
to have been occupied by the Rev. John
Burne (1562), the first incumbent after the
Reformation, and by his successor in 1574,
the Rev. Andrew Blackhall, who was also
supposed to minister to Cranstoun and
Newton.   The Rev. Andrew and his son
figure in connection with "ane musick
schooll in Musselburgh," to which King
James VI. "of worthie memory" gifted
300 merks furth of the newly-erected lordship of Newbattle, formerly the patrimony
of the Church.   Possibly Mr Andrew Blackhall, minister of Aberlady, and son of the
minister of Inveresk, was moved by the
numerous examples of the facility with
which sacred benefactions then changed
hands.   Mr Adam Colt reports of him at
a later date, "the said Mr Andro has
sauld and disponit the said pensionne, sua
that the parochine and the schooll is frustrat
of his Majestie's gift."   It was after the
Duke of Lauderdale, of happy recollection,

presented the Rev. Arthur Millar, a staunch Episcopalian, on 9th June 1680, that a manse was erected on the present site, the ground being provided by the town. What became of the vicarage or its proceeds is an interesting question. Mr Millar was deprived for declining to follow the example of the Vicar of Bray. He refused to pray for William of Orange and Mary Stewart as King and Queen. He afterwards became Bishop of Edinburgh. In 1740 the Rev. Frederick Carmichael was presented by the Duke of Buccleuch and received with grumbling. He is chiefly remembered by the sun-dial still adorning the manse garden, and bearing an inscription in Latin to the effect that "Time flieth faster than the East Wind." He left for New Greyfriars', Edinburgh, in 1747, and died five years later.

The history of Scotland touches that of Inveresk at many points, and hardly a great event but has its connection with the parish. Some time before 1668 Sir

William Sharpe, son of the prelate who was butchered on Magus Moor, acquired Stoneyhill, that famous camping - ground of armies, with its ancient manor-house, now long vanished. Six years earlier the father had been made Archbishop of St Andrews, with all the solemnity and splendour of Anglican ritual; the gentle and scholarly Leighton, inducted to New-battle in 1648, being consecrated at the same time Bishop of Dunblane, Hamilton becoming Bishop of Galloway, and Fair-foul Bishop of Glasgow. In the early days of 1662 Musselburgh saw such a sight as had been unwitnessed for a century. Three high dignitaries of the Church were received in the ancient burgh of regality, with all ceremony and rever-ence, on their journey to take up the duties of their dioceses. Three only, for Leighton, ever averse from display, had left them ere they crossed the Tweed, to avoid a public entry into Scotland. Corporations welcomed them, nobles and lairds met them on their way, and their reception was a blaze of colour. Through Fife the progress of the Archbishop was a triumph. David Leslie, now Lord Newark, rode in his train, remembering Dunbar. With an earl on either side, and 800 horsemen for guard of honour, Sharpe doubtless shared the sentiments of Henry of Navarre, who deemed Paris well worth a mass. Did no premonitory shudder run through his veins as they crossed the open moor, from which the earliest glimpse is caught of the ruined towers of St Andrews? It was from a visit to Stoneyhill the Primate was returning, seventeen years after that memorable journey, when Balfour of Burley, Haxton of Rathillet, and their less noted fellow-assassins, stopped his coach and slew him with innumerable wounds upon the moor. The tragedy of 3rd May 1679 found its echo in Musselburgh. On 19th June the Council, " in respect of the present troubles, occasioned by the rising of the disaffected partie in arms in the West, condescend that there be a guard keeped nightly within the burgh of Musselburgh and Fisherrow." Seventy of the inhabitants had accordingly to turn out at the tuck of drum each night, and various members of the Corporation and others were appointed commanders. Drumclog had been fought less than three weeks earlier, and exaggerated versions of the defeat of the terrible "Claver'se" would pour in.

In November the Duke of York, afterwards the last *de facto* Stewart king, rode through the loyal town. While at Holyrood he would frequently be seen in the parish; but little record of his coming and going now remains.

The outstanding incidents which moved Scotland during the fourteen years between the Revolution and the death of William in 1702 do not seem to have affected Inveresk to any great extent. In the reign of Good Queen Anne the seething excitement of the capital doubtless made itself felt, and Musselburgh would suffer by the Union no less than

other east coast towns. The opening up
of the New World gradually diverted the
growing foreign commerce of the country
to places rising into importance upon the
Clyde.

Of the first of the three ill‑fated at‑
tempts to restore the supremacy of the
Stewarts, Musselburgh would learn only
from the fishermen who had been dis‑
turbed by the great French fleet under
the Comte de Fourbin as it came to
anchor off Fife Ness. On board was the
Chevalier. The seamen would tell how
they heard the firing of far‑off cannon,
and, when morning broke, found the
horizon white with the sails of the Eng‑
lish ships in hot pursuit. Then, when
they expected such a fight off the Bass
and the May as gladdened the watchers
on the steeple of Crail in the golden days
of stout Sir Andrew Wood, the French
crowded on canvas, and with a favouring
wind melted into the thin sea haar and
were gone.

The '15 evoked wider interest, for Fife across the Firth was in an uproar after Mar's landing there by stealth and the result of the great hunting on Deeside. Stirring stories of the Master of Sinclair's raid on Burntisland and his seizure of arms would revive old warlike instincts. Then came the outwitting of the fleet again, and Borlum's conveyance of the Jacobites in the boats of Crail, Anstruther, Pittenweem, and Elie to the level shores from Aberlady to North Berwick ; the march of the Chevalier's followers west to Leith ; their gallant defence of the port against Argyle, and the march back again east to Seton. Some faint echo of it all is found in perturbed Minutes as to setting of guards and the levying of money.

Once more, in the '45, the Town Council are constrained by " ane order from His Majesty's Advocate " to take measures against the Jacobites. With what will they carried them out is a forgotten secret. Many were, no doubt, but luke-

warm supporters of the House of Hanover.
As things stood, they had no alternative
but to obey orders on the 9th of September in that famous year. Accordingly
an embargo was laid on all boats in the
harbour and in the bay, and a guard set
upon them. They were drawn up above
high-water mark, their rudders, oars, and
sails carried off, the streets and roads
patrolled, " vagrant persons that cannot
give a sufficient account of themselves "
apprehended, and all householders, burgesses and not burgesses alike, turned
out as " wairned by the officer " to keep
watch and ward in the schoolhouse at
Fisherrow. No delegation of duty was
allowed unless for " a very lawful excuse "
to the captain of the guard for the time.
The day after the first muster of the warlike householders, as " wairned," Prince
Charlie left Perth, and soon news came
of his having passed the Fords of Frew.
Less than a week later the reality of
war was brought home to the town when

the panic-stricken Hanoverian Dragoons, in wild terror of an enemy who was still at Corstorphine, dashed madly across the old bridge in the hope of escape from the clans. Edinburgh fell without a blow, while the City Fathers were seeking advice as to a fitting answer to the Prince's summons. Charles Edward entered the palace of his ancestors in triumph : King James VIII. was proclaimed at the Mercat Cross, and the windows of the tall lands in the High Street and the Lawnmarket burst into a white spray of fluttering handkerchiefs. The women had lost their hearts to the Prince Regent even before they saw him : two-thirds of the men were Jacobites for choice. The more advanced school of Presbyterian ministers and embryo ministers, those who played cards and were to be seen at the theatre in later years, were Whigs. One of them, still a youth, was to be the most famous occupant of Inveresk Manse ; another to write the 'Tragedy of Douglas,' and so

out-rival " Wullie Shakespeare " in the
estimation of enthusiastic countrymen.
The High-Flyers, or rigid Calvinists, were
Hanoverians too. Jupiter Carlyle, then
but twenty-three, with all the world before
him, gives an admirable picture of the
time. The forty - two volunteers from
Dalkeith, who hastened to display their
valour against Prince Charlie while he
was yet a name to them, were ordered
to take up their quarters in the old High
School of Edinburgh. The contingent
was outdone in numbers, if not in bravery,
by the noble hundred furnished by Musselburgh to join a force of 180 Seceders and
70 excisemen which had been called for
to reinforce the warlike citizens of the
capital. Unlike their ancestors of the
turbulent old town, most of these were
unacquainted with firearms. Meantime
each dissembled his fear of filling a
suicide's grave should the order to shoot
be given. Oblivion has scattered her
poppy over the adventures of the Mus-

selburgh men, except in so far as the
doings of the composite force of Hanoverian irregulars is concerned. Of these
we have curious glimpses, and judging
by certain incidents, Mansie Waugh does
not seem to have been an exaggerated
type of the class. Fortunately for the
gaiety of nations, the hour for action
came : the Highland host was rapidly
approaching. It was Sunday the 15th
of September. The fire-bell " jowed," and
at the sound the congregations "skailed"
with true Presbyterian alacrity. Female
relatives, forgetting the mother of the
Gracchi, fell with one accord upon the
necks of the volunteers and wept. The
situation was critical, but help was at
hand. The apostolic but degenerate successors of those Covenanting clergymen
whom Montrose had treated with regret-
table disrespect, and Leslie with unwill-
ing obedience, " conjured the volunteers,
by whatever they held most sacred," to
remain at home. Being douce men, un-

desirous of creating unnecessary vacancies in the eldership, they obeyed. The friends of the future Dr Carlyle eventually adjourned to a certain Lucky Turnbull's, adjacent to the Tron, to await the event. Before that, and while still drawn up in the Lawnmarket, Jupiter, with his usual sense of the humorous, remarked how " in one house on the south of the street there was a row of windows full of ladies, who appeared to enjoy our march to danger with much levity and mirth. Some of our warm volunteers observed them, and threatened to fire into the windows if they were not instantly let down, which was immediately complied with."

" So daring in love, and so dauntless in war,
  Have ye e'er heard of gallant like young Lochinvar ? "

If the volunteers found discretion the better part of valour so did their superiors. The Lord Justice-Clerk betook himself to Brunstane ; the Solicitor-General had pressing affairs elsewhere ; even His Majesty's

Advocate, having issued his imperious orders to Musselburgh Town Council, disappeared for the time.

It was on the 20th of September that the skirl of the pipes was heard in the Parish, and breathless boys tore into Fisherrow with the news that Prince Charlie at the head of his army was passing New Hailes. By the time he reached the site of the forgotten chapel that stood at the end of the Market Gate, every window and door was thronged to see " the lad that was born to be king."

> " I heard the pipes play clear,
> And Charlie is my darling,
> The young Chevalier."

From Fisherrow, then but a very large row of houses, the fishermen, less numerous than in the preceding century, but all kept on shore by the measures adopted at the instance of the Lord Advocate, thronged to cheer their Prince. We know how he looked to the Jacobite imagination, with the glamour of high hope about him, and the memories of the glory and the tragedy of his line. It may be interesting to see him through the eyes of his opponents. One beheld a tall and handsome youth, " of a fair complexion, . . . on his breast the Order of the Star of St Andrew." Another records " a slender young man about five feet ten inches high ; of a ruddy complexion, high-nosed, large rolling brown eyes, long visage ; his chin was rounded, and mouth small in proportion to his features . . . in Highland dress, with a blue sash wrought with gold coming over his shoulder, red velvet breeches, a green velvet bonnet with gold lace round it."

It was the summer of the White Rose. The Prince won all hearts by his demeanour. He acknowledged smilingly the shouts of welcome from the men : he bowed to his horse's mane in recognition of the greetings of the fair. Maybe some grim Whig smiled sourly when he saw the broom-head purloined by a Celt and carried on a pole, as the Dutch admiral in the days of the Merrie Monarch lashed a besom to his mast-head in token of his determination to sweep the seas. He would note the rude accoutrements, and remember the trained regiments of the German Lairdie. Meantime Cope moved up to Prestonpans by the low road near the sea, where the white rose and the red bloom side by side under the blue skies of June. From the slopes beyond Fa'side the Prince looked on the position chosen by the English, and found it so strong as apparently to preclude attack. He posted 500 men in Tranent kirkyard, lest his foe should break through and dash on Edinburgh. The future minister of Inveresk was perched on the top of Prestonpans steeple, and acted as an intelligence department to his friends the Hanoverians. But both the youthful Carlyle and Cope were deceived. In the grey of the dawning the Highland host surged down like a mountain tarn that has burst its barriers. The

Camerons swept over the guns. When the notorious dragoons recovered their senses they were half-way to Berwick. In five minutes all was over.

> " When Johnnie Cope to Dunbar came,
>   They speir'd at him, ' Where's a' your men ? '
> ' The deil confound me gin I ken,
>   For I left them a' in the morning ! '
>   Hey Johnnie Cope are ye waukin' yet,
>   Or are your drums a beatin' yet ?
>   If ye were waukin' I wad wait
>   To gang to the coals i' the mornin' ! "

So in rollicking song with the ring of flying hoofs through it, as in tradition informed with a sarcasm not unkindly, the Hanoverian general lives on when many a greater man has long been forgotten. Charlie slept that night in the hospitable house of Pinkie, and then rode for the first time up the broad main street, planted with two rows of trees, in which were lamps, to be lighted in winter. From the town to the bridge there was a walk, also planted with trees, and fenced off from the carriage-way. At his coming the Prince had followed the old kirk road that passed under the shadow of S. Michael's, then on to Newbigging about half-way down, and doubled back again to pass in front of Inveresk House. Whatever may be the truth as to the use of Pinkie for the wounded in earlier conflicts, there is little or no doubt that those stricken on the field of Gladsmuir were ministered to there. Everything that humanity could suggest was done for their relief by the kind and clement heir of the Stewarts, in striking contrast to the action of the Butcher Cumberland when the position was reversed in the following year.

Once more on Hallowe'en the Prince Regent slept at Pinkie, his life-guards escorting him, while the army encamped at Dalkeith on the first stage of the march to Derby. Musselburgh knew him no more for ever, except in immortal song, and in memories cherished long beyond the generation that once saw him with the eye of sense.

The '45 was the Burgh's last experience of actual warfare, though during the Napoleonic struggle it resounded with the tramp of armed men and the crackle of musketry. The extensive wooden barracks have gone, leaving no trace of those stirring days except in doorways closed by masonry where once they stood. For a moment it seemed as though the ancient days of invasion were come again, and the plan of clearing the country before the foe must once more be carried out. On Candlemas night, 1804, the beacons blazed through the Borderland, and the men whose ancestors had so often ridden under the moon gathered like them at the summons. But St Abb's Head remained dark, and the false alarm that would otherwise have roused Scotland to the northmost county was checked in time.

In the 'Reminiscences of a Scottish Gentleman,' commencing in 1787, interesting glimpses of the Burgh and of its inhabitants about this period are given.

While at the "scholastic establishment of
Mr Taylor in Musselburgh," then attended
by the sons of the best families in Scotland,
the author had opportunities of seeing the
neighbourhood at an era that to-day seems
as remote as "the Forty-five." There is
the once famous, now forgotten, duel in
which Captain Macrae killed Sir George
Ramsay on the Links, even as there is the
presentation by a group of strolling players
in the Town Hall of "The Last Days and
Execution of Louis XVI. King of France."
Europe had not yet recovered from the
rage and horror which the Reign of Terror
inspired, and when Tam Paterson, the
town drummer, and Jeemy Guild, the
baker's ne'er-do-weel 'prentice, bore the
body of the murdered sovereign across
the stage, the effect produced upon the
more emotional part of the audience was
similar to that chronicled with regard to
Mansie Waugh on his first visit to the
theatre. Then there is in these pages the
march of regiments either on their way to

embark at Leith, or passing to and from other stations : the parades of troops encamped on the links both of Fisherrow and Musselburgh : the sports of the severe winter of 1794-5 when the roads were well-nigh blocked and the mails passed through the town in post-chaises drawn by six horses, the guard inside with the letter-bags piled round him, while from the Esk came the shouts of curlers and the ring of steel on the ice. There is much else set down with the vividness only possible to a contemporary.

It is in the quiet fields of literature and in the eminent men who made it their home that the interest of the Parish henceforth centres. Under Dr Carlyle the Manse had been the resort of the *literati* of the age ; and a brilliant gathering they were, not to be equalled now. David Hume, Adam Smith, Adam Ferguson, Dr Robertson the historian, Dr Blair, Tobias Smollett, and many others took part in those earlier *Noctes Ambrosianæ* of the era of Guy

Mannering. Concerning Jupiter himself it is unnecessary to say anything more here. His autobiography is a classic, and no one can tell his tale so well as himself. He died in 1805, the date upon the steeple of the building that by no desire of his rose on the denuded site of old S. Michael's. That venerable and hallowed church would at least have remained what we should now call an ancient monument had Dr Carlyle had his way, and in that event there would have been a possibility of the restoration of the holy house where our fathers praised God through so many centuries.

The parish had other attractions for the cultured and the leisured than the society of its minister. It had a calm lowland beauty all its own; it was near the capital but not of it; it was full of historic and antiquarian interest; the scream of the sea-mew mingled with the curlew's call within its boundaries. Its breezy links were the haunt of a select company of golfers; there

the Royal Company of Archers shot for the
Silver Arrow of Musselburgh. It became
famous for its schools. The stately villas
of Inveresk, always an aristocratic village,
and the quaint dwellings of the dual town
on either side of the Esk, attracted those
whose strenuous work was over or who
sought lettered calm. The closing half of
the eighteenth century and the earlier half
of the nineteenth was the Augustan age of
the ancient town and its suburbs. Distinguished men in varied walks of life
made it their abode for a season; the
grey memorial stones in the kirkyard tell
how many won a rest there at last whose
names are not yet forgotten.

Judges and generals, admirals and
authors, crowd that century. David Dalrymple, Lord Hailes, member of a family
that has contributed more distinguished
men to the Scottish Bar than any other
save that of Dundas, spent his happiest
years at New Hailes. Scotland boasts
no more painstaking historian than the

learned judge who was the contemporary
of Kames and Monboddo and of "Weir
of Hermiston," Lord Justice-Clerk Brax-
field. Gilbert Stuart, the historical essayist,
sojourned within the limits of the Parish.
There were the homes of the makers of
history no less than its chroniclers. Lord
Clive, Sir Ralph Abercromby, and Admiral
Sir David Milne, one of a family of distinguished sailors, come within its annals.
Sir Walter Scott knew it well, and not
only composed some of his most martial
verse there, but drew upon its characters
and products in his novels. Distinguished
lawyers like Lord Stair and Lord Eskgrove
made it their residence. The White House
was occupied by the Countess of Hyndford,
who brings it in touch with Stevenson's
finest story, even as the Parsonage is associated with "Marmion." For the Countess
was no other than Janet, daughter of
William Grant, Lord Prestongrange :—

> "I am Miss Grant, *sib* to the Advocate,
> You, I believe, are Dauvit Balfour."

Even so, a name in the list of heritors in 1807 conjures up visions of Alan Breck, and the Wood of Lettermore, and much beyond.

The claim of Inveresk to direct literary fame centres in David Macbeth Moir, the Delta of 'Blackwood,' author of the inimitable 'Mansie Waugh,' a classic rich in humour, produced in the alembic of a poetic mind from genial observation of the humbler classes of Musselburgh, while the Burgh still kept the quaint characteristics suggested rather than pictured in Mr Ainslie's 'Reminiscences.' Dr Moir's career covered the first half of the nineteenth century. He was born on the 5th January 1798, and died on the 6th of July 1851. It was the busy life of a country practitioner who grudged no toil in the performance of his duties. His output of literary work was marvellous when the scanty leisure afforded him is considered. To 'Blackwood's Magazine' he contributed three hundred and seventy

articles. How high he stood in the affection
of his countrymen was shown when he appeared on the platform in Edinburgh to
lecture at the Philosophical Institution.
His subject was "The Poetical Literature
of the Past Half-Century," a criticism of
contemporary poets by a poet. Busy as
he was, his verse reflects a calm, placid,
and meditative mind, keenly susceptible to
the beauty of nature and moved by the
sadness that lies at the heart of things.
Tears and laughter are never very far
apart. The same pen wrote 'Mansie
Waugh' and 'Casa Wappy'; the same
genius pictured for posterity the mirth-
provoking adventures of the "Dalkeith"
Tailor and the tranquil charms of autumn
twilight in 'Sweet Eskvale.'

Delta was on terms of friendship with
the *literati* of a time which ranks high in
the record of Scottish literature. Mr Galt,
the author of the 'Annals of the Parish,'
came to live at Eskgrove when Moir was
twenty-five, and left 'The Last of the

Lairds' to be finished by his friend while he went abroad. Christopher North and others of the "Blackwood" group visited Musselburgh to enjoy the Doctor's society. With the poets and poetesses, authors and authoresses of the South, he was on terms of correspondence. More than sixty years have gone by since he was laid to his rest in the churchyard on the hill; but his work lives, and his place on the roll of Scottish men of letters is secure.

In the atmosphere of that age when the voices of war and civil strife had at last been stilled, and Inveresk, untouched by industrialism, her beauty still undimmed, dreamed of her past, this sketch may well conclude. The wild roses bloom by the river and up the way the English came till you reach the ruined castle on the hill. The Firth lies sparkling in the sunshine; on the London Road a cloud of dust and the faint echo of a horn tell where the mail-coach passes. The cushats are calling their melancholy croon from the Shire-wood, above which old S. Michael's lifted its heaven-pointing tower through so many centuries from the summit of the holy hill.

" All music voiced about the woodland spaces
    Sounds to one sacred note ;
Peace, like a bird, hallows the lonely places
    With gentle throbbing throat.

No noise of grief or cry of lamentation
    Breaks upon that still coast,
Rather the holy hush of consecration
    Before the uplifted Host."

II.

THE RIDING OF THE MARCHES

THE RIDING OF THE MARCHES.

PART I. ORIGIN AND PURPOSES.

THE ceremony of perambulation of boundaries persists with singular vitality. Other rites less ancient have long gone into desuetude, and are remembered only by the antiquary and the student while this endures, even where one of its original purposes has been forgotten and another has become unnecessary. In Britain it is found under varied names. In the Border towns the Common Riding, sometimes associated with incidents of warfare, round which time has thrown a glamour of romance, fires year by year the patriotism of the indwellers of those ancient settlements; in lowland Scotland certain venerable burghs ride their marches at longer or shorter intervals with an enthusiasm that seems to strengthen as the generations succeed each other ; in England there are many parishes that regularly " Beat the Bounds."

The roots of the custom are deep bedded in the soil of an immemorial past. Beyond the era of the Roman *Terminalia* and kindred pagan rites, beyond the days when Jacob set up a pillar of covenant with a heap of stones at Galeed as a boundary which neither he nor Laban should overpass, the quest might be followed through strange lands and amid forgotten peoples.

In these pages later beginnings may suffice, and it appears unnecessary to anticipate the coming of the Northmen and the conditions on which land was then held. That similar pre - feudal conditions still exist in the Udal tenures of Orkney and Shetland is partly explained by the identification of ancient Scandinavian and ancient German proprietary uses, and, for that

matter, of ancient Celtic custom.[1] It is
needless to go beyond the confines of an
adjoining county to study these, for close
beside us, in the Burgess Acres of Lauder
and in Lauder Common a perfect survival
is to be found of the primitive cultivating
community. There, according to a return
made to the House of Commons in 1870,
"within the bounds of the royalty of the
burgh are 105 separate portions of lands
called Burgess Acres," varying in extent
from half an acre to three and a half acres,
these being the absolute property of individuals. It is shown that no one had
been admitted a burgess who was not
owner of one of these acres; that, in the
common, extending in all to 1700 acres, a
portion varying from time to time, but
recently about 130 acres, had been given
in allotments, one to each owner of a

[1] 'Village Communities in the East and West.' Henry
Sumner Maine. London : John Murray, Albemarle Street,
1871. Skene's 'Celtic Scotland,' Book III. c. iv.

Burgess Acre, for cultivation by him, and that the remainder of the moor had been used for grazing purposes. On the pastoral part of the common each burgess resident within the burgh grazed two cows and about fifteen sheep, and each widow of a burgess one cow and about a dozen sheep.

Lauder is typical of the primitive state of things, a specimen unique in its perfection, though traces of what had been yet exist, not only in Britain, but in countries far removed. Maine is doubtless right in his contention that "the Indian and the ancient European systems of enjoyment and tillage by men grouped in village communities are in all particulars identical." Individuals would come together for mutual protection and for the society of each other. As nomad tribes they wandered about following the chase, an instinct that still survives. Then they settled down to a pastoral life, growing rich in flocks and herds and beginning to till the soil of which they had taken permanent

possession. Each would reclaim and cultivate an "acre" in the ground they had
mutually marked out for their own ; their
cattle grazed on the pasturage that belonged
to all, while watch was kept for the common
benefit against the incursion of reivers and
caterans. In days when a strong king
ruled, and the bracken bush kept the cow,
a single watchman would be sufficient, as he
was again in the eighteenth century. Delta
tells that he remembers the Musselburgh
herd sounding his horn in the early morning and the kye trooping slowly out of the
closes at the call. In the evening they
came home in the like order, and each
turned off into the familiar entry of its
own accord. So in the villages of Switzer-
land and of the Bavarian Highlands you
may see them still and listen to the tinkle
of their bells as they take their road.
When portions of the land came to be let
or feued the proceeds found their way into
what was known as the Common Good.

The introduction of the feudal system

into Scotland was undoubtedly for benefi-
cent and patriotic purposes, which purposes
it served until, with the death of the Regent
Randolph, Earl of Moray, in the old house
by Pinkie Gate, the country entered on
a period of turbulence under the weaker
rulers who followed. Then the feudal chiefs
usurped power wherever they could, and
the story of the Stewarts is one long
conflict between the king, backed by the
common people on the one side, and the
majority of the fierce and predatory nobles,
many of them in the pay of England, on
the other. The instincts of the latter, kept
in check by King and Church with more
or less success through several centuries,
found unrestricted scope when the Reformers triumphed with their help, and
the scandalous seizure of church property
of every description threw great parts
of the country into practical paganism.
The overlord of the feudal system was a
valuable protector ; but in a barbarous age
he had his weaknesses, and one of these

was for ground that did not belong to him. When lands were unenclosed, as in earlier times they were, encroachment was easy and natural, and it required the combination of a strong arm with a watchful eye to prevent alienation. In many instances the commons mysteriously disappeared. What had been such formed the subject of a grant by those who assumed a title they did not possess. When a town was under the protection of a lay lord of the barony it had to preserve its rights against him. Against outsiders he might be trusted to maintain and defend them. "Commons remained or disappeared at his will, or according to his strength to carry it into action. In fact, he was titular owner merely and lord superior; in law, he was superior and owner in one. But the law was brought into harmony with fact by the grant of the property right, and his retention of his superiority in the common land of the town. The town, armed with the grant, took upon itself the protection of its property. But in an age of continual strife a trading community occupied a secondary place against the barons with their retainers, whose business was war and continual thought arms."

Such, then, is the explanation of the common lands and the common good of the venerable Burgh of Regality lying under the shadow of the holy hill of Inveresk, as through the long centuries of the past it lay under the special protection of "Halie Kirk." The very word "acre," once so familiar in the holdings of the parish, is still remembered in isolated instances. The Rood Acre, the Acre of the Holy Cross, has preserved its identity, and though in the absence of the foundation charter absolute certainty as to the meaning of the name is impossible, it was in all likelihood set apart towards the support of the rood altar which would stand on the rood loft in S. Michael's Kirk. The rental or the produce that the acre yielded would either supply the lights that burned there in days when light was costly, or help to pay

the chaplain who was specially attached to
it. Mr Adam Colt refers to another, "the
aiker, callit Thomas' Aiker," the teinds of
which, with those of Hudescroft, an appel-
lation like so many more within Great and
Little Inveresk, reminiscent of the mediæval
Church, were part of the vicarage stipend.
Punlars Acre, near a bed of clay at the
eastern boundary, is a further instance,
while everywhere the Saxon term, "God's
Acre," that

> ". . . consecrates each grave within its walls,
> And breathes a benison o'er the sleeping dust,"

is a very beautiful example of the old
nomenclature and the old tenure.

The Rood Acre would probably have
passed out of popular ken but for the fact
that it bounded the town's possessions, and
that a divot has been cast there ever since
the procession took its glittering way round
the Marches.

If evidence of the early system of holding
in the parish, beyond what is supplied by

analogy and place-names, were required, it could be found in such records as that which tells how Thomas Smith was served heir to his father, a burgess of Musselburgh, in two ox-gates of the lands of Inveresk and two and a half acres in the moor of Inveresk, together, it is interesting to read, with the office of hereditary miller in the Shire Mill, with the Mill Acre.

Musselburgh was a populous community when the great Roman station on the hill was in its glory, and even, on the evidence of archæological discoveries, in the old days before that. It held of no overlord, save the Church, in the person of the Abbot of Dunfermline, till the Reformation overwhelmed the ancient order, and the king gifted the superiority to John, Lord Thirlestane, all but Pinkie of the Setons, which was specially excepted. Whether the Abbots of Dunfermline encroached on the original possessions of the Burgh there is no evidence to show. In all likelihood these remained intact, save for such as

were set aside by the community for the
service of S. Michael's and its subsidiary
chapels. Possibly the commonty may at
one time have extended southwards beyond the limits of present perambulation.
"Seven hundred acres in the fields of
Inveresk" were certainly divided in 1756
among the adjoining proprietors ; but these,
long part of the moor of Inveresk, were
then outwith the Burgh lands, if they ever
came within them. Probably they did not,
for at the north end was the stagnant
bog called the Howe Mire, from which
malarious vapours rose by day, and over
it by night eerie lights sought to lure
the belated wanderer. It was drained
after the partition through the enterprise
of the lairds interested. No procession is
recorded to have passed beyond the Rude
Acre in that direction. The Shire Mill,
however, at the top of the Shire Haugh,
now enclosed within Dalkeith Park, was
within the liberties. Before the Reformation the Abbot of Dunfermline had gifted

it away, and it remained the property of Sir James Richardson of Smeton till 1627. It was burned down in 1827, and finally sold in 1828 by the magistrates to the Duke of Buccleuch, and with it went the banks of the Esk upward on the east side. It may be taken that although the two baronies, called Great and Little Inveresk, comprised an area considerably greater than the parish of to-day, it was not the Burgh that suffered from encroachment.

As has been indicated, the feudal system, which came into Scotland in the days when Saint Margaret, the sister of Edgar Atheling, heir to the throne of the Confessor, ruled Scotland with her warlike husband, Malcolm Canmore, "operated generally for the people's rights and liberties." [1]   Under the king and queen the change was gradually effected that a free people, remaining free, might be organ-

[1] See 'A Short History of Feudalism in Scotland,' by Hugh B. King.   Edinburgh and Glasgow : William Hodge & Co.   1914.

ised for defence. It was a necessary hypo-
thesis of the system that all land belonged
to the king, even as all honours flowed
from him; and one of the earliest known
charters is that granted in 1124 by
Malcolm and his queen to her favourite
abbey, Dunfermline, and confirmed with
certain additions in 1152 by that Sair
Sanct for the Crown, David I., and by
Bulls of Pope Lucius III. in 1182 and
Pope Gregory IX. in 1234. It was this
charter that divided Inveresk into the
two baronies. David II., in 1354, in turn
executed a charter in favour of four
burghs, holding of the abbey. Of these
Musselburgh was one. It confirmed all
their ancient rights and privileges as
burghs of regality. So it held till the
Reformation turned the world upside down.
But again, after more than a century had
gone by, John, Earl of Lauderdale, of the
line of Thirlestane, came to the rescue with
a fresh charter to the same effect as those
that went before, and this too was ratified

by King Charles the Second shortly after
the Restoration. The superiority eventually passed by purchase into the hands
of the noble family of Buccleuch, in the
days of the Duchess who wedded the Duke
of Monmouth and kept royal widowed
state at her Palace of Dalkeith till her
death.

The ceremony of Perambulation of
Boundaries was preponderatingly religious
in its observance, till the overthrow of the
ancient Church in the sixteenth century.
The institution of Rogation Days is attri-
buted to Mamertus, Bishop of Vienne
(France) in 452, when that city was sub-
jected to a terrible ordeal through volcanic
eruptions, fire, and the incursions of ter-
rified wild beasts. The bishop set aside
three days before Ascension Day as a
solemn fast, during which processions
with litanies were to be made throughout
the diocese. The practice was taken up
by other dioceses, and came into vogue in
England and Scotland in course of time.

It was three centuries after Mamertus till it was recognised at Rome.[1]   It may possibly have existed in the Church before the striking events of 452 called attention to Mamertus's solemn observance with special reference to them, for the missionaries of Christianity adapted to higher uses the customs they found prevalent.   However that may be, Rogation Days and their observance are referred to in the most ancient records of the Church of England. They are still called Gang-days in parts of northern England, the same name they bore in the reign of Alfred the Great and of Athelstan.   Then they were *Gang daegas,* with the alternative of *Gebed daegas* or

[1] Cf. Harford & Stevenson, 'Dictionary of the Prayer Book.' Pitman.

'The Annotated Book of Common Prayer,' edited by Rev. J. H. Blunt, M.A., F.S.A. Rivingtons, 1876.

'Documentary Annals of the Reformed Church of England from 1546 to 1716,' by Edward Cardwell, D.D. Oxford University Press, 1839.

'History of the Book of Common Prayer,' by Francis Procter, M.A. (18th Edition). London : Macmillan, 1889.

'Church of Our Fathers,' Hart and Frere. Vol. IV. London : Murray, 1908.

I

Prayer Days, reflecting their dual signifi-
cance. Pictures have come down out of
old time of such processions. The ritual
exists, and shows the manner in which they
were kept so early as the eighth century.
There was the bearing of a crucifix, of the
shrine containing the relics of the saint,
the chanting of litanies, the stopping at
the crosses which marked the boundaries,
while all the people knelt and begged
God's forgiveness for their sins.

In the Sarum Missal may be found the
Collect, Epistle, and Gospel for Rogation
Days. These were not retained in the
Prayer Book. There was, however, a
Homily in three parts for the days of
Rogation Week, and an " Exhortation to
be spoken to such parishes where they
use their perambulations in Rogation
Week for oversight of the bounds and
limits of their town."

From time out of mind, then, these
perambulations had been made, and the
Litany, with the 103rd Psalm (in its met-
rical version consecrated by usage as a

Thanksgiving immediately after celebration of Holy Communion in the Church of Scotland), had been sung, together with the 104th.

Religious processions were abolished in England in the year in which the battle of Pinkie was fought, the first year of Edward VI. ; and as they had come into use again under Mary Tudor, Queen Elizabeth's Injunctions of 1559 repeated the prohibition of them almost word for word. From this, however, was excepted the Rogation March. The words are interesting as showing how both the religious and secular purposes of it are recognised :—

". . . For the retaining of the Perambulation of the Circuits of Parishes, they shall once in the year at the time accustomed, with the Curate and the substantial men of the Parish, walk about the Parish as they were accustomed, and at their return to the Church make their common prayers.

"Provided the Curate in their said common Perambulations used heretofore in the days of Rogation, at certain convenient places, shall admonish the people to give thanks to God

in the beholding of His benefits for increase and
abundance of His fruits upon the earth, with the
singing of the 103 Psalm : *Benedic anima mea*, &c.

"At which time also the same Minister shall
inculcate these or such sentences, 'Cursed be he
which translateth the boundes and dolles of his
neighbours,' or such other order of prayer as
shall be hereafter appointed."

A further example is contained in the
exhortation printed as sequel to the Rogation Day Homily. It is set forth that the
chief object of the procession is that of
asking God's blessing upon the land and
its fruits : " yet have we occasion second-
arily given us in our walks on these days
to consider the old ancient bounds and
limits belonging to our township."

Nor was feasting forgotten when the
round was accomplished, any more than
now. In the quaint language of an old
writer in Mary Tudor's troubled reign,
"in game wyke called Rogasyon weke
they whent a prosessyon with baners in
dyvers places, . . . and they had good
chere after."

In Izaak Walton's Biography we are told of the saintly Hooker: "He would by no means omit the customary time of Procession, persuading all, both rich and poor, if they desired the preservation of their parish rights and liberties, to accompany him in his perambulations."

The double meaning of the rite, then, clearly appears. In those "old ancient days," when each man's hand kept his head, and when war and civil commotion were everyday events, and none felt sure that he would see another sun go down, things unseen were more constantly in mind than they are amid the comparative security of life to-day.

"It was not only as clad in weeds of peace or the livery of their gilds our countrymen wended in long-drawn processional array amid the shady lanes and the green meadows, or along the city streets all hung with silks or tapestry, but also when girt in iron and sword in hand, with death glancing upon them on

the battlefield, that they cried unto the
Saints in Heaven, and besought their
prayers with God."

There are many references in the Acts
of the Parliament of Scotland to the
perambulations of bounds, from the days
when David I. and William the Lion conducted them in person, down to those when
powers were given to a commission to ride
disputed marches in the shire of Ross,
in the year when the great Marquess
of Montrose was sweeping like a meteor
across the land to inexplicable extinction
at Philiphaugh. In one of these it is
laid down that in causes of perambulation no person is to be received upon
the inquest but men having heritage of
their own, who know the bounds of the
lands, and dwell within the shire, or at
least within the next four shires.

When the Church was dominant, and
religion permeated the thoughts and lives
of men, perambulation was pre-eminently
an act of praise and prayer. That has

passed with the crosses where the procession knelt. The elimination of the
religious element cannot be counted for
gain; and it is permitted to us to hope
that it may yet be restored to its proper
place in the proceedings. It is, strangely
enough, the other aspect alone that is
remembered, the safeguarding and vindi-
cation of proprietorial rights. The hurri-
cane of the Reformation in Scotland swept
utterly away the once predominant feature.
Probably the Reformers were of opinion that
any procession whatever, in which Churchmen had taken the chief part, was "idol-
atrous." But even sports, dear to the
heart of the people, such as the much
denounced "Robert Hude," lingered on
despite excommunication and malediction,
till the iron had entered into the soul of
the commons. The perambulations they
could not kill, even if they would. In the
general scramble it became more necessary
than it had yet been to guard with vigil-
ance the possessions of a burgh or parish.

The crucifix and the sacred relics might go, as go they did under the most drastic penal legislation; but full armour and flashing sword - blades took their place, with a champion to settle in single combat the fray that might else render desolate many homes. The sole object now was to keep in remembrance the March stones, solemnly set up so long before, or the place where the broken crosses stood, and to preserve the rights of property. As in France the whipping of youths at the limits of the parish is, or was, a prevalent practice, so in Britain. At S. Mary's, Leicester, there was a pleasing variation of the mnemonic rite. There the parish officer on his appointment was conducted round the frontiers of his new domain, and had his head thrust into a hole dug for the purpose. While in that ignominious posture the shovel was applied to his person with sufficient vigour to ensure the operation acting as a further incentive to memory. Where a stream formed a march, the ducking of boys naturally suggested itself by way of substitute for the usual castigation.

The Riding of the Marches would become at Musselburgh far more urgent after the Reformation began, so far as the precautionary aspect of the ceremony was concerned. Formerly the whole power of the Church was arrayed against any infringement of the rights of the lands and burghs under its protection. That withdrawn, every baron and laird of high or low degree sought what advantage he could, even as the common people plundered the shrines, and took the lead from coffins and from roofs. The primitive instinct that " he shall take who has the power, and he shall keep who can," always emerges in times of revolution, and is equally strong in democracy and in aristocracy. But the burghers were too much accustomed to the march of armies, English and Scottish, not to be able to hold their own against all - comers. Unfortunately over that interesting period little light shines. The Kirk - session records only begin in 1651, and those of the Town Council are in hardly better case. The earliest mention of the Riding is in 1682, which is accounted for by the fact that now the Church had no part or lot in the procession, and that the regular burgh records only begin three years earlier, though traces exist from 1605, and more coherently from 1635. The archives and charters are said to have been carried off and destroyed by the English under Lord Gray, when he gave the town to fire and sword five months after the battle of Pinkie. Possibly many of them perished in Hertford's earlier "visitation." But, as the Council in 1711 resolve that the Marches be ridden "with all the usual marks of antiquity and respect and grandor," it is obvious, if such evidence be still required, that it was an ancient institution. It had come to be associated with the morning of " S. Lauretto's

Fair," whatever that was. It may possibly have been associated with the crowds of pilgrims who came together to that chapel and hermitage. The dates in October, or exceptionally in November, of the earlier recorded Ridings, seem to point to connection with S. Michael, the patron saint of the parish, whose figure was to be found of old on the burgh seal and arms, and ought to be restored by a town which is justly proud of its past. That the date of the perambulation should, despite the fact that the Rogation Days come before Ascension, be fixed for the Saint's Day, is in accordance with Scottish practice. That day was kept in special honour : it was a holy day, when all work was suspended, and men were free to take their part in the procession. Thus in Dumfries, where the Archangel is patron, the ceremony, when observed, took place on 1st October. Linlithgow, also associated with S. Michael, is truer to the Rogation Days. There the Riding takes place on the first Sunday after the Whitsun Fair. Lanark is in similar case. The celebration is on the last Wednesday of May (Old Style). In not a few of the Ridings are to be found traces of earlier rites than the Christian, and having stronger affinities with Beltane than Rogation-tide. Into that fascinating subject there is not here space to go. The cell at Loretto was in existence for little more than a quarter of a century, and that the name superseded that of S. Michael and survived the chapel for a hundred years, serves to show how famous was that place of pilgrimage to which kings and queens resorted when in special anxiety during its brief existence.

In 1830, the first year of William IV., the Sailor Prince, the date was altered to June; in 1852 it was again June; but in 1873, in 1893, and in 1914 it was changed with more apparent reason to the morning of S. James's Fair in August, the principal holiday of the year, held from time immemorial.   On that day for centuries back to a period when shooting at the Butts was obligatory, and they were set up beside the churches, the Royal Company of Archers usually competed for the venerable Silver Arrow of Musselburgh, on the Links. The only festival which rivalled it in the ancient Burgh was Beltane, and that has fallen into desuetude. The Chapel of S. James stood at the end of the Midraw watching over the Market-place and the Town Cross, and looking west to the Tolbooth over the square.   It was doubtless the Town Chapel, open for constant prayer in a praying age, and resorted to like the Liebfrauenkirche of Nuremberg to-day by those who brought in with the sunrise their produce for sale under its shadow.

When first the Ceremony comes into actual view in written record in the days of the last Stewart King, thirty-two years after Cromwell's Ironsides lay upon the Links and his horses were stabled in S.

Michael's Kirk on the hill-top, it is not difficult to recall the scene. Proclamation had been duly made, the town bell had been rung from the hoary steeple that alone escaped Hertford's incendiarism, and there gathered on the crisp October morning in the Market-place and round the Cross the men on the burgess roll, each on his horse, in warlike array, his sword by his side. The seven incorporated trades, the old Trades Guilds of the Burgh, hammermen, tailors, shoemakers, baxters, gardeners, weavers, and butchers, in their Scots blue bonnets and wearing cockades, mustered at their lodges or at the doors of their box-masters. When all were formed up, they trotted to the Square, each Guild with its captain and adjutant at its head and the banner emblematic of the craft waving proudly over it. The cordwainers alone possessed a king, Crispin, whose regalia is still preserved in the Edinburgh Municipal Museum. Meantime the town piper was playing martial music, and the

stalls doing a merry business, especially in
stands of ribbons for the young and fair. A
shout would go up from the crowd of country
folk and townspeople as down the steps of
the Tolbooth, built from the consecrated
stones of Loretto, came in stately progress,
first the town officers with their ancient
Brabant spears, and then the two magistrates in their curled wigs, the senior bearing the sword of justice, the councillors
following two by two, all of them armed
for the fray that might once have impended
on such a mission.   There rode up the
champion, his vizor down, prepared to
challenge to single combat any who dared
dispute the extent of the Burgh's jurisdiction.   The piper struck up a wilder
and more defiant strain, the rough-riders
clattered out of the gathering place, and
after them, with more measured step, followed the procession, eastward past the
Chapel Gavel — the gable of S. James's,
adorned now with fleshers' hooks for the
display of meat, and clustered about at

market time with booths, even as was S. Giles' in Edinburgh all the year with krames. On beside Pinkie, which had then just passed from the Setons to the Earl of Tweeddale, but in which the old family had left the eldritch portrait of Lady Jean, the Green Lady, who even yet, it is whispered, glides down the narrow stair and walks with noiseless footfall the long gallery when the night is still and deep. Massive and imposing, the great pile reared its age-worn tower and stretched out straight on either side of the fortalice of the Abbots of Dunfermline. Over the waste ground then belonging to the town, and purchased three-quarters of a century later by Sir Archibald Hope of Craighall, rose the beautiful fountain on which, for a time, the fine old house turned its back. In it the poetical imagination of Dr Moir and others before him saw the design of a mitre, and traced the outward expression of the sympathies of the Setons generally and of the Lord Chancellor in particular.

Leaving the ruins of Loretto on the other
hand, they would go to West Pans, where
the first sod was cut and the challenging
shout, "It's a' our ain," rang out. Then,
ascending Edgebuckling Edge, they paused
at the White Brig over the Ravensheugh
Burn on Lord Tweeddale's lands of Drummore to repeat the ceremony, and so along
the ridge to an enclosure which, in the
end of the eighteenth century, belonged to
William Spence of Felton Green "next to
Pinkie Field." They had been travers-
ing ground on which the English army
encamped on the night of Black Saturday.
The next halting-place was at what in
1790 came to be an enclosure pertaining
to Richard Fisher of Loretto. It lay at the
head of the Cottage Lane, east of the
present Grove Street, once called Sycamore
Grove, and marched with the lands of
Pinkieburn on the south-east and those
which came to belong to Lord Eskgrove
on the west. From that point they would
probably return and canter along beyond

K

Newbigging, then turn back past Inveresk
House to the Cross of Inveresk. From
letters written by the Provosts of 1830
and 1852, the former to the Hon. North
Dalrymple and the latter to Mr Colt, the
successive occupants of the property so
long possessed by the Colt family, the
Cross would appear to have been within
the present policies.[1]   It is recorded in
1790 that it stood " near the original entry

[1] The letter written by Provost Campbell to Mr Colt
runs as follows :—

" Provost Campbell of Musselburgh respectfully intimates
to Mr Colt that it is the intention of the Town Council to
ride along the ancient Marches of the Burgh on Tuesday
the 29th of June current.

They will, as on former occasions, require access to the
grounds of Inveresk, to cast turf at the old Cross at Inveresk, where a stone of three feet long is placed near the
foundation of a wall at the original entry to Inveresk
House, and it is trusted that Mr Colt will allow the Gate
to be opened.

" Provost Campbell requests also that Mr Colt will have
the goodness to allow the procession to pass along the walk
from Inveresk through the grounds to the north Gate, so
as to have egress by it.

" Care will be taken that not the slightest trespass is
committed.

" TOWN HALL, MUSSELBURGH,
          25th June 1852."

leading to the house of Robert Colt, Esq.,
where a stone of about three feet long is
placed near to the foundation of the wall
of the said original entry, which stone
formerly was called the Cross of Inveresk,
and was anciently fixed or placed in the said
stone wall and evident to ocular demon-
stration." The casting of the divot here
was known as "the Auld Cross Cut."
According to Mr Alexander Inglis, who
rode as a boy in 1830 and acted as turf-
cutter in 1852 and 1873, the cut was made
beside a stone in the roadway between the
stables at Inveresk Gate and Inveresk
House, which conflicts with the evidence
contained in the letters. The stone is
stated by Mr Inglis to have been cylin-
drical in shape and sunk in the ground
and to have had in its upper surface a
hole which had formed a socket for an
iron cross. According to the 'Musselburgh
News' of 12th May 1893, it was "believed
to be still *in situ*." There is grave reason
to doubt the identity alike of site and stone

with those mentioned in the protest. That the pre-Reformation Cross of Inveresk was of iron is, to say the least, extremely unlikely. A stone occupying the position referred to by Mr Inglis has been examined. It measures but 22 inches long, and is hollowed into a basin with a rim 5 inches wide at the top. Tradition avers that upon it the coffin was rested when a funeral passed up to the church. It may confidently be averred that the Cross of Inveresk is still to find. Most probably the stone anciently so known, and other parts of it, are buried in the ground near the spot where Knox's "rascal multitude" overthrew what it regarded as "ane monument of idolatrie."

From S. Michael's Cross the horsemen trotted south - east again to the Rood Acre, south of the Orchard Dean or hollow at Pinkieburn. A field in the vicinity is still known as Mary's Brae, and associated in the popular mind with the surrender on Carberry Hill. In all

likelihood it bore its name long before the
unhappy Queen rode, with Kirkaldy by her
side, down the ancient Roman Way.   An
enclosure at the east end of the village
of Inveresk, at Pinkiehill Farm, appears
to have been visited on certain occasions.
This was distinct from the Rood Acre.
Thence the early riders would pass down
to the waterside and so to the Dove
Croft south of Inveresk Lodge and the
Manor House,—a point long omitted, but
taken up again in 1873 at the foot of
the Windy Wynd, on information given
by Sir Archibald Hope.   Then those seven-
teenth-century riders put their horses to
the Brae and rode up to the South-West
Cut, about fifteen yards to the west of
the south entrance to the churchyard.   It
would be interesting to know how the
tradition of the silence that fell there on
the cavalcade originated.   Was it a thing
of yesterday—a reverent desire to refrain
from disturbing the peace of the Acre
where the dead sleep sound, or an earlier

tradition of an awestruck race? For just beyond the wall of the earliest kirk-yard rose the *Duine Sidh* — the Fairy Mound — from whose summit, ere the fairies came, the sacred fire blazed at Beltane and on The Night of Fires. Straight onwards, down what is now a service road, the procession went to the head of the Tail Race, where in 1750 and for long after the "Walke Miln" stood. While the Sheriff or Shire Mill still belonged to the town, it too was visited, as were the Mill Haugh and the Mill Rigg contiguous. The river flowed nearer Monktonhall, and the ride was not so lengthy as it now appears. They then wheeled about and cantered back to the Dove's Croft, which was a piece of ground consisting of about two and a half acres, lying to the south of the Old Bridge, and doubtless so named from a columbarium of the monks of Dunfermline. Was it here the Rude of the Brigend stood? When the river was low the horse-

men took the ford; when the Michaelmas
spate roared down, they passed the gates
on the bridge to the south corner of the
Bogle Hole or Terrors' Croft, where a
divot, in the end of the sixteenth and
greater part of the seventeenth century, would be cast with trepidation. It
was the Devil's Acre, as the churchyard
was God's, and was left uncultivated and
ungrazed. None would willingly visit it
after nightfall, and strange sights and
sounds were the portion of those whose
evil fate led them to its vicinity. There
witches and warlocks convened, and
xxvj^s viij^d appears in the rental of the
Abbey of Dunfermline as paid for it by
Bessie Froge,—a name sufficient to war-
rant John Knox burning its possessor if
she were old and ugly. In the earliest
records the point where the procession
passed is referred to as Stonnie Hill
Park Dyke. It is only in 1790 that
the name Bogle Hole appears. The possession next visited was the Common

Myre, which was feued in later days to the famous historian, Lord Hailes. It adjoined his lordship's lands of Whitehill, otherwise Newhailes. There, near the Chapel of Saint Mary Magdalene and by the side of the burn, once stood an ancient cross. Last of all, in the words of an early Protest, "in presence of the said Magistrates and the said attendants, the said Notary and Procurators and Witnesses crossed Magdalen Bridge and proceeded to Brunstane Mill and Milnhaugh in order to ascertain the superiority thereof, and of the eight - ninth parts of the Multure of all Grain Grinded or manufactured at the said mill of Brunstane : But on arriving at the Outter Gate or entry leading to the said Mill, we ffound the same shut, and John Thomson, Tenant at Easter Duddingston, standing in the Inside of the Gate, and when admittance was demanded to pass to Brunstaine Miln : He answered, that he was authorised by Lord Abercorn's Doer,

Mr Walter Scott, Writer to the Signet, to refuse the Town of Musselburgh admittance to the said Mill : Whereupon the said Mr Harry Guthrie, Junior, as Procurator foresaid, asked and took Instruments in the hands of the said Notary Publick subscribing in presence of the said Witnesses." In the Riding of 1790, at which the incident above recorded took place, the Notary proceeds : " And in like manner the said Procurator took Instruments in my hands at the several Boundarys of the Burgh's Territorys before specified, and which our Boundarys we ffound all now Inclosed on both sides without any Incroachments on either side."

This record is interesting as bringing the town into contact with the father of Sir Walter Scott, the Saunders Fairford of 'Redgauntlet,' the cautious old Clerk to the Signet, who feared that his illustrious son would prove "but a gangrel scrapegut"; nor when, as Lord Abercorn's

"Doer," he authorised defiance of the worthy magistrates, did he dream that one day it would be among the proud memories of Musselburgh that that son should write a canto of 'Marmion' within its territory, and draw upon its characters in 'The Antiquary' and the list of its products in 'Rob Roy.'

A similar experience at Brunstaine Miln had occurred forty years earlier, when the Riding of the Outmarches of the Town's Common Ground took place in 1750. The cutting of the turf had begun at the east end of the Common, next to "Revelshaw burn," and the procession came at length to the western extremity, "with ane intention to cast a fioll or divot upon that part of the town's Common lying above Brunston Miln, But found same was Inclosed by a stone dyke and the Gate shut upon us, so that we could not get access thereto : Therefore ye said William Watson [the notary] in name and behalf foresaid protested that ye Person to whom the said dykes belonged should be lyable not only for the value of said peece or part of Town's Common Inclosed as said is, But for all Cost, and Raites, damages and expenses as accords of the law."

Through the two centuries and more of which actual record remains, the ceremony changed but slightly, except that the date came to be August — S. James's Fair superseding S. Michael's Day for the celebration. The appearance of the Riders would alter with the years : we have a glimpse of tall hats with black cockades in the middle of the eighteenth century. Once steel headpieces and breastplates had been worn. Wigs and powder, sur-mounted by cocked hats or velvet caps, and the blue bonnet of the yeoman, gave place in turn to less picturesque adorn-ment. A military band superseded the town piper ; the Seven Trades Guilds merged into a display of growing and expanding industries, which altered from generation to generation till the great

procession of the present time is reached,
and there is included, in the train who
follow on, a pageant of the centuries
through which the town, amid many
vicissitudes, has played its part in the
annals of Scotland.

THE first part of the foregoing historical
sketch concluded with the defeat of the
Scottish Army at the disastrous battle of
Pinkie in 1547 ; the second ended on a
note of profound peace three centuries later,
when the country had settled down to a
period of calm after Waterloo. At the
time it was written there was no thought
of the cataclysm of blood so soon to deluge
Europe. The German menace had long
threatened : but a conflict under modern
conditions must be of a character so de-
structive as to be almost unthinkable, and
the idea of its indefinite postponement
seemed to be generally accepted. There
appeared at the moment nothing likely to

precipitate a struggle fraught with issues
the wisest dared not forecast.

In the ancient burgh the preparations
for Riding the Marches were practically
complete. The story of Inveresk and
Musselburgh was to pass before the eyes
of the onlookers in a pageant in which the
best-remembered episodes of twenty centuries were to be represented, and in the
second part of the procession contemporary conditions of life within the boundaries of the parish were to be illustrated.
The varied ceremonies of the day had
been planned in detail and the actors
chosen. The costumes to be worn in the
pageant had either been made at home or
were on their way to the town.

The old Scottish chroniclers are prone
to record premonitions of coming evil.
Douglas dreams his eerie dream before
Otterburn; the midnight stillness of the
High Street of Edinburgh is broken by
the ghostly roll-call from the Mercat Cross
of those who are to fall at Flodden. No

such warning was vouchsafed to Britain in
1914, though ere autumn was over the
words of the prophet Joel were recalled
to the minds of many ; so that had Jhone
Leslie, Bishop of Rosse, and that still
more delightful historian, Robert Lindesay
of Pitscottie, lived in a later age to write
the record of the Great War, they would
not have lacked such ferlies as those with
which they embellish their respective nar-
ratives of the days of the Stewarts. Even
as in Pitscottie's record of the early reign
of Queen Mary, he tells that Mr George
Wisheart " saw also a great misty and
smoky cloud arise in the south-east and
move forward till it came just above
Dunpender Law, beside Haddington ; and
having stayed there for a quarter of an
hour, it divided itself so that the one part
stood right above Haddington ; the other
half moved north-west, till it came above
the Kirk of Inverask, and there appeared
like blood descending out of the firma-
ment ; " so might he now have chronicled

blood-red sunsets and gory moons barred with black, and revelled in such tales as that of the mysterious drum tapped by no mortal hand on board the *Royal Oak*, when the Fleet was cleared for action ere the German ships surrendered—the drum of Drake beating to quarters as in the spacious days of Queen Elizabeth—when the Armada threatened England with as great a peril, and hearts as stout went dauntlessly to meet it. Few would then have questioned what many still believe, the vision of the hosts of heaven under S. Michael, leader of the armies of God, fighting for the right, turning by a miracle the tide of battle against overwhelming odds.

Just as the most beautiful pictures are those which were never painted, and the sweetest songs those no mortal voice has sung, so the most picturesque of all the Ridings was that which was never to take place. Yet in the realm of imagination it endures—a pageant passing in a world

of dreams. There were to have been the
Pictish hunters who tracked the wolf, the
bear, and the fierce white cattle of the
forest of Caledon ; there the Roman
charioteer, the centurion, and the soldier,
vestiges of whose sojourn in the camp
upon Inveresk Hill may still be seen.
Malcolm Canmore and Saint Margaret were
to have progressed through the parish as
in the days when they came to kneel before the Altar of Our Lady in S. Michael's
Kirk, and William to have had borne before
him his famous banner with " the ruddy
lion ramp'd in gold." The Great Synod of
1242 was to have been recalled by Bishop
de Bernham of St Andrews with his attendant clergy. The Abbot of Newbottle
with his monks in their white cassocks,
black scapulars, black leather girdles and
white hoods, were to pass again the Milns
they established. Sir William Wallace,
with Crystal of Seton, Robert Lauder and
his band, were to tread the road they followed when they thundered to Dunbar.

There would have been Randolph, Earl of
Moray, with his successor, the Earl of Mar,
and the burgesses of the honourable town.
The connection of Musselburgh with the
Low Countries would have been recalled by
a crowd of Dutch women and Dutch men,
and the fifteenth-century guilds were to
follow.

There, too, would have been many more
of whom mention has been made in the
foregoing pages — the Hermit of Loretto,
Mary of Lorraine and her daughter—that
other Mary for whom so many went gladly
to their death—

> " Yet none for you of all that bled
> Grudged once one drop that fell,
> Not one to life reluctant said,
> Farewell "—

and about her the Four Maries of history, song, and romance, with attendant
pages and squires. The " Auld Enemies,"
in the persons of Somerset and his followers, were to ride along the street,

where at their behest the red cock crew so fiercely; and there, old feuds forgotten, would march beside them Arran and the stubborn Scottish spearmen whose "dark impenetrable wood" broke the chivalry of England. Cromwell would have been seen again with his Ironsides, passing his camp upon the Links and his quarters in Inveresk House; and to the skirl of the pipes Prince Charlie, with Lochiel and Elcho, and the kilted clans, march by Pinkie and recall the glories of Gladsmuir and of Holyrood.

There, too, would have been the lawyers of the Augustan Age, who helped to shed a lustre on Inveresk—Lord Hailes the historian, Lord Binning, and Lord Eskgrove. Then, after the Highflyer coach that spanked down from London in the earlier decades of last century had rolled more demurely on its way, the Seven Incorporated Guilds would have completed the tale of the centuries.

While those who lived through it remain,

the tension and excitement of the week-end which ushered August in will not be forgotten. Every hour brought news of events which were to change the destinies of nations ; but not until Britain actually declared war on Germany, on Tuesday the 4th, was it comprehended that the hour so long foreboded had struck at last.

As in the case of many other celebrations, great and small, to which a peaceful people were looking forward, it became evident that the Marches could not be ridden in 1914. Even had it been fitting to proceed while the fate of the Empire hung in the balance, it would have been impossible. Men and horses alike would have been wanting. The Territorial Forces had been mobilised ; recruits were flocking to join the Army and the Navy ; those who were to have followed Prince Charlie, or formed the train of Queen Mary, were already in touch with the realities of modern war.

Musselburgh found its traditions of

Napoleonic days revived, and seemed to
have passed into a century - old atmosphere.   Those who lay awake o' nights
heard the tramp of unknown hosts and
listened to the distant rumbling of cannon.
Cavalry were seen fording the Esk at midnight as in the romantic years of long ago.
The shores of the Forth were guarded and
patrolled ; soldiers were stationed in various
quarters.   West Pans had its extemporised
fort ; the river mouth had another ; and so
on east and west.   Railways and bridges
were under close supervision, and in the
early days of autumn there was a spice
of adventure in approaching after nightfall some youthful sentry whose zeal in
unaccustomed circumstances tended to
outrun discretion.

As in the period depicted in ' The
Antiquary ' and ' Mansie Waugh,' the possibility of invasion was always present,
especially during these first years.   No
one knew what had been or was being
planned beyond the North Sea, and such

information as was available to the authorities was strictly censored. History was
repeating itself. At any moment of the
day or night might come the orders to
the honest burghers to betake themselves,
with such chattels as they could carry, to
some fastness beyond the Pentlands or
the Lammermuirs. Again might the successors of Monkbarns and Mansie have to
arm in hot haste. The formation of a
volunteer corps had afforded an outlet for
the patriotic fervour of those who found
themselves from various causes unable to
join the armies in the field. It need not
be doubted that, had it been actually put
to the test, either by a landing on Gullane
Sands, where David Balfour saw Alan
Breck on board the *Thistle*, or by such
a false alarm as that which on Candlemas
Day 1804 roused the Border counties,
and brought the men of the Selkirkshire
Yeomanry to Dalkeith without drawing
rein, the old spirit would have flashed
up.   As to the likely outcome, it were

doubtless wisest to quote the words of
the aged gaberlunzie, Edie Ochiltree :—

"Troth, I kenna : an' they come sae
mony as they speak o', they'll be odds
against us. But there's mony yauld
chields amang thae volunteers : and I
maunna say muckle about them that's no
weel and no very able, because I am something that gate mysell : but we'se do our
best."

No beacon glow, or its modern equiva-
lent, lighted the hill-tops to disturb the
community, whose closest experience of
hostilities was at midnight on April 2
to 3, 1916, when a fleet of Zeppelins
throbbed over the town. It was known
to be on its way an hour or two before,
and was therefore expected. When all
lights were extinguished, the inhabitants
waited on with a tense excitement and a
nervous thrill never before experienced.
Crowds flocked to the hill of Inveresk
and to the Links, disregarding warnings
to remain under cover. A mysterious

humming sound growing and waning : a crash, and then they saw the red glare shoot up from Leith, where a warehouse burst into flames, and listened awestruck to the explosion of the bombs which fell upon Edinburgh, where the Castle seemed the centre of attack. A month later lights went out again ; but the raid was arrested, and Musselburgh heard no more the actual din of hostile aircraft.

From the first months of war the feeling of indignation against the German conduct of the conflict was intense. Wild stories of espionage on the part of those to whom Britain had given a home for years obtained ready credence. The authentic reports of atrocities in Belgium, which, being perpetrated by a people nominally Christian, and long understood to be civilised, seemed more terrible than the doings of the Alans and Sueves, Huns and Vandals, who poured in upon the corrupt Empire of Rome, drove the

youth of Britain to the colours. A
Recruiting Committee had been formed
in Musselburgh immediately after the
outbreak of hostilities, and great meet-
ings were held, at the close of which
scores of men who had never thought
to take part in fighting were enrolled.
Recruiting offices were opened on both
sides of the Esk. The gravity of the
situation was not at first fully appreci-
ated, owing to the censorship, but events
like the Fall of Namur, and the Homeric
struggles that marked the Retreat from
Mons, followed in the early days of
October by the capture of Antwerp,
made it apparent that every British subject must exert his utmost effort.

Gradually the burden pressed more
heavily. Streets were darkened and windows shrouded, that no ray of light might
guide the Raiders of the Air or of the
Ocean. Traffic was reduced to a mini-
mum by the withdrawal of men, horses,
and vehicles for service elsewhere. There

was hardly a household that was not
kept on a rack of anxiety as to the fate
of its members in some theatre of the
war, and many were plunged into mourn-
ing by news from France or Belgium,
Gallipoli or Mesopotamia, Egypt, Africa,
or the sea. In the terrible railway
accident at Gretna the parish suffered
heavily.

The fishermen of Fisherrow rose gal-
lantly to the occasion, and the hardships
and privations they endured, and the
part they played in protecting the coasts,
is known fully to the Admiralty only,
though from time to time thrilling tales
of encounters with the enemy close to
our shores reached those at home. The
spirit that animated the hardy seamen
who fought under the stout old Scottish
Admirals, Andrew Barton of that Ilk, and
the still more famous Sir Andrew Wood
of Largo, lived on in those who manned
the Fleet, from super-Dreadnought to
mine-sweeper; and had the Germans ven-

tured in strength so far afield, a battle
off the May could have had but the
same result as that which the folk of
Fife watched from Fifeness, and the
roofs and even the steeple of Crail, for
one long summer day and part of another,
when the *Yellow Caravel*, or the *Yellow
Frigate*, as it is better known in romance,
and the *Queen Margaret*, brought at last
the three great warships of England in
triumph to Dundee.

Meantime, in the churches on both sides
of the Esk, intercessions for the success
of our arms were regularly made. In the
Parish Church of S. Michael, round which
the tide of war had so often surged, and
in which masses had been said for the
souls of those who fell at Bannockburn
and Flodden and Pinkie, and in many a
minor fray, prayers were offered daily.
United services, when the great building was thronged, marked the anni-
versaries of the Declaration of War
during its continuance. Money was given

with unstinted generosity towards every
scheme that ministered to the welfare of
those who were fighting in one way or
another for King and Country, and for
the homeless refugees who sought safety
from the invader. Organisations for help-
ing in other ways speedily sprang up,
and hostels for disabled men were established.

As the years passed on, with the end
still seemingly remote, the ruthless submarine continually reduced the already
depleted merchant service, and the re-
quirements of the Army and Navy in the
way of men and material restricted the
productivity of countries even where they
were not actually devastated. The injunction went out to cultivate every possible foot of ground. It was cordially
obeyed. Those who had never handled a
spade found congenial occupation in the
work of the garden and the field, and the
town set apart allotments for all who
chose to take them.

Meantime the industries of the Burgh adapted themselves to circumstances. Of the three greater concerns to which alone it is possible here to refer, the oldest, the Net Factory, established almost a century ago by the inventor of the loom for weaving fishing-nets, and carried on for the past seventy years by Messrs J. & W. Stuart, naturally found its business paralysed by the opening of hostilities. None more loyally gave their services than the fishermen of Scotland and England, and they were immediately engrossed in the preparations for defence of the coasts. The export trade was stopped. Circumstances, however, gave a new outlet for patriotic endeavour. The submarine menace had to be countered, and one means of doing so was by the wire nets which were so successfully used. Large numbers of these were made at Esk Mills, and the firm also supplied considerable quantities of netting of every kind for all the Fronts. In conjunction with the Elswick firm of

Sir W. G. Armstrong, Whitworth & Co., Limited, parachutes for star-shells were produced without stint.

The Inveresk Paper Company's contribution to the prosecution of the struggle was naturally chiefly from the ranks of its employees. When the war began these numbered 595, of whom 477 were men and 118 women. When the Armistice was signed there were but 207, made up of 169 men and 38 women. Active service, the making of munitions, and the like had claimed the rest. So far as is known, 15 of the men had fallen in the field and 3 were killed in the Gretna disaster.

The Steel Wire Mills of Messrs Brunton played a very important part, and, to meet the demands upon them, were continuously extended. The firm have been good enough to supply some indication of the wide range of their activities, and from this it appears that, when war was declared, they were already in a position to

produce stream-line wires and tie rods for
the rigging of aeroplanes; that the Admiralty sent their technical expert to the
mills to conduct experiments and tests;
that they made all the wires and all the
special wire-fittings for the first rigid air-
ship built in this country, and that thereafter all wires and cables used in the
construction of rigid airships so built were
manufactured at their mills. There, too,
was produced the turbine blading used on
Admiral Jellicoe's flagship, the *Iron Duke*:
there they experimented as to indicator-
nets, which they not only made themselves
but instructed others how to make. Another variety of net which they invented
and patented was that for aerial protection, erected over the King's private
apartments at Buckingham Palace and
many other important buildings. They
also mention that they were the principal suppliers of paravane rope, and that
when the Armistice was signed they were
turning out a special section of steel for fuse

collars in quantities sufficient to make five hundred thousand shells per week.

With a suddenness as dramatic as its beginning, the end of the war came. Germany struck her last blows, and under them the Allied armies reeled for a moment. That frenzied effort failed, as ultimate failure, despite temporary success, had really been certain from the beginning. The Armistice was signed on S. Martin's Day, 1918. The Imperial Crown fell from the brow of the Hohenzollerns, and that of the Hapsburgs rolled beside it in the dust. The Fleet that, directed by a bolder brain, might in 1914 and 1915 have disputed the empire of the seas, was surrendered and devoted to an end far more ignominious than that of the Spanish Armada. The Confederation moulded by Von Bismarck and Von Moltke into the mightiest military power in the world crumbled into fragments, and anarchy threatened for a time those States in which ordered Government had ruled every phase of life. The tragedy was practically complete.

The ground-swell of the great storm which had brought to the surface of European politics strange creatures from the depths might take years to exhaust itself; but from the moment that truce was called Britain was free once more to think of her domestic concerns and pick up the broken threads of abandoned projects.

In Musselburgh and Inveresk the changes were not less striking than elsewhere. Many of the best and bravest, living on in the hearts that loved them, would return no more. Many were maimed and broken. Yet not even those who suffered most regretted the sacrifice.

It was indeed in many ways a different world in 1919, and it was impossible that the arrangements for the Riding of the Marches made five years before should stand altogether unchanged. Instead of a pageant devoted to the history of two

M

thousand years, it was decided that the part it would have played should be taken by a display representing the forces which had gone together to victory. The band of the Comrades of the Great War would be followed by the men of Edenhall Hostel —the Pinkieburn of pre-war days — and these by mounted officers. Then would come British artillery with their guns and Italian artillery with theirs. The pipe band of the Comrades of the Great War would head men from each of the Scottish regiments, who would be followed by Frenchmen, Belgians, Italians, Australians, Canadians, and New Zealanders, and men of the Flying Corps. To sailors of the Allied Navies would succeed Red Cross Nurses and representatives of Women's Army and Navy Auxiliary Corps. The Parish Church of Inveresk had the suggestion made to it that, in memory of fallen Presbyterians, it should present a flag or banner to be carried in the procession, and a similar invitation was sent

to the Roman Catholic Church with regard to the commemoration of men of the
Ancient Faith who fell fighting for the
same cause. If the proposal were accepted
the flags would be returned to be preserved
in time to come in the churches, each of
which is dedicated to the Archangel represented in the Arms of the Burgh as
triumphing over the Dragon of Evil.

As far as possible the other features of
the postponed celebration were to remain
as originally designed, all sections of the
community promising to do their utmost
to make the occasion worthy of the traditions of the venerable town.

So again, after the five years of storm
and stress that have come between, this
chapter may surely close upon a note of
peace with the bells that peal in celebration of the Treaty of Versailles ringing
out the thousand wars of old.

APPENDIX

APPENDIX.

RIDING OF THE MARCHES OF THE COMMONTY OF MUSSELBURGH.

PLACES WHERE PROTEST TAKEN AND FFIOL OR DIVOT CAST.

1682. **S. Lauritt's Fair: Tuesday, 16th October, at 8 a.m.**

First record of Riding in Town Council Minutes. Races next day.

1711. **S. Lauritt's Fair : exact date not given.**

First day Riding.
Races next day.
"Ridden this year with all the usual marks of antiquity and respect and grandor."

1732. **S. Lauritt's Fair, 18th October.**

No details extant, except in the account of an affray between the tailors and the weavers mentioned in the note appended hereto (pp. 195 and 196).

1750.   16th October.

(1) East end of Common next to " Revelshaw
Burn."

(2) South side of Do. next to Pinkie Field.

(3) Rood Acre at east end of Inveresk.

(4) " Walke Miln."

(5) Stonnie Hill Park Dyke,

and

prevented at part of Town's Common
lying above Brunston Miln, which was
found enclosed by stone dyke and closed
gates.   Protest taken there.

1764.   2nd November.

(1) East end of Common next to " Ravenshaugh Burn."

(2) South side of Do. next to Pinkie Field.

(3) Rood Acre as above.

(4) Shire Milnhaugh.

(5) South end of Park belonging to the
minister's manse.   Where a piece of ground
was by the Bailies and Council added to
the said park for an yearly rent.

(6) At the Waulk Miln.

(7) At Stoneyhill Park Dyke.

(8) Within the inclosure called the Common
Myre ffeued by the Town to Sir David
Dalrymple of Hailes, Baronet,

and

prevented at Brunstain Miln, enclosed as
aforesaid.

1790. 12th November.

Here first notice taken in the Protests of convening at the Market Cross: of the presence of "the two Magistrates, the Councellers, and many reputable Burgesses—inhabitants of said Burgh": of the seven Corporations of Tradesmen belonging to the Burgh, all in proper array, with their several banners emblematical of their several employments—all on horseback, preceded by the Town's sergeants and a select band of music.

This time they started out westward and cut the sod as follows :—

(1) In Penman's, now Archibald Cochran's, Park, lying to the south of Stone Bridge of Musselburgh—the piece of ground commonly called The Dove Croft—consisting of 2 ac. 2 r. and 30 falls lying near the Damside.

(2) Corner of Lord Drummore's ffeu.

(3) Inclosure belonging to William Spence of Feltongreen which marches with Pinkie ffields, divided by a stone dyke, hedge, and ditch.

(4) Inclosure belonging to Rich. Fisher of Loretto, marching with lands of Pinkie Burn on the south-east and Inclosures of Lord Eskgrove on the west parts.

(5) In Inveresk near the original entry leading to the house of Robert Colt, Esq., where a stone of about 3 feet long is placed near to

the foundation of the wall of the said original entry : which stone was formerly called the Cross of Inveresk, and was anciently fixed or placed in the said stone wall.

(6) The Rood Acre, now the property of Sir Arch. Hope of Pinkie, which Rood Acre lies in an enclosure on the east end of Inveresk Village opposite to and on the south of the Mansion House of Pinkie Burn.

(7) Common Ground lying above the Stone Bridge and near the hedge which divides the lands belonging to the Waulk Mill.

(8) South corner of the Boglehole, bounded by lands of Stoneyhill.

(9) East end of the Common Myre adjoining Newhailes.

(10) Prevented at Brunstane Mill from entering (as before).

1809.   25th October (Jubilee Year of King George III.)

Assembled at west end of road contiguous to Fisherrow leading to new Stone Bridge of Musselburgh.

Usual gathering with the seven Corporations, banners, &c.—all on horseback.   Proceeded eastward along High Street to

(1) Lord Drummore's feu (now Wm. Aitchison of Drummore) and near West Pans.

(2) Inclosure some time belonging to William Spence (see 3 in previous Riding), now to Sir John Hope, Bart.—now divided by a stone dyke only.

(3) (No. 4 in previous Riding), now designated the Entry, commonly called the Cottage Lane, on the east side of Union Place, leading to an enclosure some time belonging to Richard Fisher, now to Sir John Hope, Bart., divided by a hedge and ditch from an enclosure on the south of the property of the said Sir John Hope, which now belongs to Sir David Rae, late Lord Justice-Clerk.

(4) The Dove Croft (No. 1 in previous Riding).

(5) The Cross of Inveresk ("which stone formerly was called the Cross of Inveresk"). (No. 5 in previous Riding.)

(6) The Rood Acre.

(7) The Sheriff Miln (not visited in previous Riding) with the Mill Haugh and Mill Rigg contiguous.

(8) The Waulk Miln (No. 7 above), a spot near to the hedge which divides the lands belonging to the Waulk Miln of Musselburgh.

(9) The piece of ground lately feued from Arch. Cochran on which the town built a Flint Mill (not previously visited).

(10) Boglehole (No. 8 in previous Riding).

  (11) Common Myre adjoining New Hailes (or Whitehill, as it was otherwise called).

  (12) Brunstane Mill. Door found open this time and notary entered and protested. Afterwards protest taken on the Mill Haugh for the 8/9 parts of the multures.

1830. 9th (29th?) June (1st Year of William IV.)

Assembled at north end of the road contiguous to Fisherrow leading to the new Stone Bridge. Six of the seven Corporations — Hammermen, Taylors, Shoemakers, Bakers, Weavers, Gardeners, and Fleshers. All on horseback.

Route eastward across new Stone Bridge to

  (1) Lord Drummore's Feu—Daniel Taylor, gardener, broke ground.

  (2) Spence's, now Sir John Hope's, Inclosure (No. 2 of 1809).

  (3) Up the Cottage Lane (No. 3 of 1809).

  (4) Penman's Inclosure (The Dove Croft) (No. 4 of 1809).

  (5) Inveresk Cross (No. 5 of 1809).

  (6) The Rood Acre (No. 6 of 1809).

  (7) The Waulk Miln (No. 8 of 1809 : the Shire Miln having been sold with the east of the Haugh to the Duke of Buccleuch). (See pp. 125, 126.)

  (8) The Flint Miln (No. 9 of 1809).

  (9) Boglehole (No. 10 of 1809).

  (10) Common Myre (No. 11 of 1809).

(11) Crossed the Magdalene Bridge and proceeded to Brunstain Mill, Miln Haugh, and Damhead.

> Turf cut at each place.

> This time Thomas Lees as Procurator, on the ground of the said Mill Haugh, requested the Marquess of Abercorn to render an account, and thereafter pay the amount of the 8/9 multures.

(12) To preserve the superiority of the property aftermentioned, they crossed at the entry leading from the High Road to the north side of "Maitland Bridge Burn" and Pinkie Pans and returned down Fisherrow and crossed the New Stone Bridge, and so to Musselburgh Links, and solemnly protested these respective properties belonged to the Burgh.

1852.   29th June.

Assembled west end of Bridge Street. Members of the Seven Corporations: also Old Youths and Caledonian Youths—Band of 7th Hussars, Town officers with halberds, &c.—no mention that all on horseback—to

(1) Lord Drummore's Feu.

(2) To properties at West Pans, held partly by Sir George Grant Suttie and partly by William Aitchison, Esq. of Drummore.

> *Note.*—This spot has not been mentioned before.

(3) Spence's Enclosure (No. 2 of 1830).

(4) The Rood Acre (No. 6 of 1830).

(5) Up the Cottage Lane (No. 3 of 1830).

(6) Enclosure at east end of Village of Inveresk.

(7) To the Cross of Inveresk (No. 5 of 1830).

(8) To the road leading past by the south gate of the Churchyard of Inveresk towards the Waulk Mill of Musselburgh and the River Esk on the north side thereof. (This is possibly No. 7 of 1830 : but see No. 10 hereof.)

(9) To the Dove Croft (No. 4 of 1830).

(10) To the Town's Common Ground lying above the Old Stone Bridge and near to the hedge which divides the lands belonging to the Waulk Mill of Musselburgh.

(11) To the Flint Mill (No. 8 of 1830).

(12) To the Bogle Hole (No. 9 of 1830).

(13) To the ground and entry from the highroad to the north side of Magdalene Burn and Pinkie Pans, held partly by Charles Dalrymple Ferguson, Esquire of Hailes, and partly by John Wauchope, Esquire of Edmondston. (This appears to be in place of Common Myre, No. 10 of 1830—which was evidently omitted on this occasion.)

(14) Crossed the Magdalene Burn by the Magdalene Bridge and proceeded to Brunstane Mill and the Miln Haugh and Damhead

there—for the purposes specified in all preceding instruments of Protest (No. 11 of 1830).

"At each and all of the several places Alexander Inglis . . . broke ground," &c., in order to maintain and secure the rights and boundaries of the said Town of Musselburgh's lands, and instruments taken.

Returned *via* Magdalene Bridge, Pinkie Pans, down Fisherrow, over New Stone Bridge to Links, where dismissed by the Provost in name of the Town Council.

1873. 13th August.

Assembled at west end of Bridge Street. Band of 1st Royal Dragoons — Corporations, Fishermen's Society, Old Youths, Caledonian Youths, Foresters, Freemasons, 1st Mid-Lothian Coast Artillery Volunteers, Musselburgh Corps of 1st Mid-Lothian Rifle Volunteers, banners, flags of the Trades, &c.—passed eastward to

(1) Ravenshaugh Burn (No. 1 of 1852).

(2) Spence's Field (No. 3 of 1852).

(3) Up the Cottage Lane (No. 5 of 1852) to field held by the Heirs of Sir David Rae of Eskgrove.

(4) To the enclosure at the east end of the village of Inveresk and south of Orchard Dean, now held by Sir Alexander Hope.

(Is this the Rood Acre? See Nos. 4 and 6 of 1852, from which the confusion may have arisen.)

(5) Thereafter to the Dove Croft, *south* of the village of Inveresk, and now held by Lady Mary Oswald and Sir David Wedderburn, or either, "being the south boundary of the burgh." This is a curious entry.

> *Note.*—This is *not* the Dove Croft of former Ridings; but seems to be somewhere at the back of the Manor House or Inveresk Lodge. It may have been part of the Common of Inveresk.

(6) To the Cross of Inveresk (No. 7 of 1852).

(7) Road leading past by the south gate of the Churchyard towards the Waulk Mill (No. 8 of 1852).

(8) Penman's Land (the Dove Croft of former Ridings) (No. 9 of 1852).

(9) Flint Mill site (mill now gone), near the Waulk Mill, now belonging to Messrs Alex. Cowan & Sons, and forming the south-west boundary of the burgh (No. 11 of 1852).

(10) Bogle Hole (No. 12 of 1852).

(11) Ground at high-road to north-east of Magdalene Burn and at Pinkie Pans (No. 13 of 1852).

(12) Common Myre (left out in 1852).

(13) Along Magdalene Bridge, &c.—as before
(No. 14 of 1852).

Same protest as usual at the Mill.

Return exactly as in 1852.

1893. 9th August.

Assembled at Town Hall. Band of 12th Royal
Lancers, Musselburgh Corps of Mid-Lothian Artil-
lery Volunteers, the Corporations, Mechanics, Free
Gardeners, Old Craighall Benevolent Society,
Fishermen's Society, Tailors, Tanners, Bakers,
Confectioners, Fleshers, Carters, Engineers,
Masons, Joiners, Stuart's Net Factory, Inveresk
Paper Company, John Young & Co., Brewers, and
others.

Passed eastward to—

(1) Ravenshaugh Burn (No. 1 of 1873).

(2) South-westward to Spence's Field (No. 2 of
1873).

(3) By Cottage Lane to enclosure (No. 3 of
1873).

(4) To enclosure at east end of village of
Inveresk (No. 4 of 1873).

(5) To the "Dove Croft" south of Inveresk
(No. 5 of 1873—a new spot visited in
that year, apparently for the first time),
described as "the South Boundary of
the Burgh." It never was the Burgh
Boundary.

(6) To the Cross of Inveresk (No. 6 of 1873).

N

(7) Road leading past south gate of Church-yard (No. 7 of 1873).

(8) Back through the grounds of Inveresk to the Flint Mill site (so long as the March was *ridden* they would canter down through the Kirk Park). (No. 9 of 1873.)

(9) Bogle Hole (No. 10 of 1873).

> *Note.*— Omission in 1893 of the old Dove Croft at end of Old Stone Bridge. It has probably arisen through the confusion of two Dove Crofts—that which figures here from early Ridings and the newly introduced "Dove Croft" at south of Inveresk. It even remained in 1873 as " Penman's Land." (No. 8.)

(10) Along Magdalene Bridge to Brunstain Mill, &c. (No. 13 of 1873—with usual Protest.)

> *Note.*—Omission of Common Myre (No. 12, as also of No. 11 of 1873).

Return as in 1852 and 1873.

NOTE.

The Riding of 1732. In the Appendix to 'The Domestic Annals of Scotland,' vol. iii., Dr Robert Chambers quotes from the 'Caledonian Mercury' an account of an affray that befell in the Honest Toun: "The Magistrates, according to ancient annual custom, had to perform the ceremony of riding round the marches of their burghal property. On this occasion they were attended by their vassals and the burgesses, to the number of 700, all of them of course mounted and in their best array. 'The trumpets and hautboys marched in front; then the magistrates and town council, followed by the gentlemen vassals, with the town standard; after them the several incorporations, distinguished by their respective shining new standards, and headed by the masters of the crafts. In this good order they marched out to the Links, making a gay appearance. But, alas! while they were marshalling, an unlucky difference arose between the weavers and the tailors, which should have the *pas* or precedency. In order to prevent effusion of the blood of his majesty's good subjects, they agreed to submit the merits of the cause to the magistrates. The tailors argued that, as the precedency had previously fallen to them by lot, no opposition could now be offered in that respect. It was alleged, on the other hand, that they—the weavers— were *Men*, and as such preferable at all events to

Tailors. This signal affront could not be digested. Accordingly, to work they went, without waiting the decision of authority; and while the weaver squadron were filing off to take the post of honour, with Captain Scott at their head, Adjutant Fairley, who acted in that capacity to the tailor squadron, directed a blow at the captain's snout, which brought him to the ground. Thus were the two corps fiercely engaged, and nought was to be seen but heavy blows, hats off, broken heads, bloody noses, and empty saddles; till at last the plea of manhood seemed to go in favour of the needlemen, who took Scott, hero of the weavers, prisoner, disarmed him, and beat his company quite out of the field, though far more numerous. It was with the utmost difficulty that the weavers got their standard carried off, which they lodged in their captain's quarters under the discharge of three huzzas: 'tis true the conquering tailors were then off the field, and at a mile's distance. The weavers allege, in excuse of their retreat, that the butcher squadron had been ordered up to assist the tailors, and that they did not incline to engage with these men of blood.'"

PRINTED BY WILLIAM BLACKWOOD AND SONS.